Stories of WEST ORANGE

JOSEPH FAGAN

Charleston   London

THE
History
PRESS

Published by The History Press
Charleston, SC 29403
www.historypress.net

Copyright © 2014 by Joseph Fagan
All rights reserved

First published 2014

Manufactured in the United States

ISBN 978.1.62619.553.0

Library of Congress CIP data applied for.

CONTENTS

CONTENTS

ACKNOWLEDGEMENTS

I would like to publicly thank West Orange mayor Robert Parisi and members of the West Orange Town Council, who bestowed on me the honorary title of official historian of West Orange Township in 2012. I am deeply grateful for this recognition because many people would be equally deserving. Mere words, however, cannot express the posthumous acknowledgment that three generations of Fagans in West Orange before me rightfully deserve for inspiring me to learn about local history. Former town historians, the late Stanley Ditzel and Abe Lando, along with many other individuals, past and present, too numerous to mention have all contributed to preserving West Orange history. I stand on broad shoulders and understand we all are carrying the torch that one day will be passed on to another generation. The enduring influences of my family roots and all these individuals have helped make this book possible.

I would like to acknowledge the staff at the West Orange Public Library for always allowing me access to their resources. I would like to thank the Downtown West Orange Alliance Board of Trustees, Chairman John McElroy and Executive Director Megan Brill for helping me to present West Orange history to the community. No acknowledgement, however, would be complete without mention of my deeply devoted wife, Debbie, and son, Joseph, whose unselfish love and constant support truly makes it all possible.

Finally, I would like to give a heartfelt thanks by the deepest measure possible to Matthew Schwartz, longtime friend Glenn Cignarella, Kathryn Healy, Beth Watner Friedman, Janet Cole and Mary Kushner, who helped

ACKNOWLEDGEMENTS

me greatly in bringing the Williams family clock mentioned in Chapter 1 back to West Orange.

This book is dedicated to the memory of former West Orange resident Dorothy Robertson mentioned in Chapter 8 (June 29, 1912–September 23, 2012), who has helped dearly in preserving West Orange history for all generations, past, present and future.

INTRODUCTION

The greatest resource of West Orange will always be its history and people. This book continues the time-honored tradition of celebrating our local heritage. Although much can be learned here, it is not intended to be a complete or chronological history of the town. West Orange is perhaps best known as the home of Thomas Edison. I have always contended that he deserves his rightful place in history, but there is so much more to West Orange than just Thomas Edison, as these stories will reflect.

This collection contains many colorful tales about West Orange that have perhaps been otherwise overlooked by history. It tells about surviving artifacts reaching back to colonial times. It sheds light on nationally known figures such as Amos Alonzo Stagg, who grew up here, and General George McClellan, who lived here. Countless books have been written on McClellan's life, but not a single one can provide new insight about the night he died in West Orange. This book contains never-before-published details by the last surviving person to have lived in McClellan's former house and shares a firsthand account by a person who was there the night he passed away. Liberace launched his career here, Eleanor and Franklin Roosevelt first discovered a romantic interest for each other here and the legendary football coach Joe Paterno got his start because of a decision made by a former school principal in West Orange.

Stories of West Orange tells of murder, tragedy, Olympic glory, curing cancer, automobile development, overcoming slavery, Wild West justice, a lion on the loose and more. It provides a unique cross-sectional view of historical vignettes scooped out from a streaming confluence flowing down the corridor of time and offers a glimpse into a place and time our grandparents once knew, like a message in a bottle cast adrift on the ocean, hopefully one day to symbolically wash up on shore in the minds of those seeking historical discovery. Ideally, this collection of stories and pictures will equally serve a purpose today to inspire many to become more aware of our forgotten past.

My personal family history spans nearly 150 years in the community, beginning with my great-grandfather Richard Fagan, who was born about 1868 and lived in West Orange. He was followed by my grandfather James Fagan Sr., born in 1901, and my father, James Fagan Jr., born in 1921. I have always endeavored to include stories from my own family history as an added layer of texture to tell about West Orange from a local and personal perspective.

It should be noted that every individual West Orange veteran can be credited with unselfish devotion in the service of our country. Each one has a compelling story equally important as the next, and all are worthy of our attention, gratitude and respect. Chapter 9 tells only about a few with some unique circumstances, and it is not intended to diminish the importance or sacrifices of countless other town veterans and their many contributions.

History, it can be said, is like meeting an old friend who knows who we are, tells us what we want to hear and leaves us to visit another day, politely reminding us of the best and worst of all our potential and constantly inspiring us to be what we can and should be. Some may say history is dead, but it is alive and well, and you will feel its beating pulse on the pages of this book.

History should not be considered the exclusive property of historians. Instead, it belongs to all of those who are aware of it. Hopefully, one hundred years hence, a yet unborn generation will look on this body of work and disregard the understood boundaries of time as they hear these voices of yesterday echoing forward into the future.

It is to that purpose and sense of vision to which this book is written to celebrate and preserve West Orange history because everything old will become new again to teach, guide and enlighten us on the road to our own self-discovery as a people, always mindful as worthy stewards of our community's heritage that our proper treatment of history will one day be the final verdict on ourselves.

Chapter 1
SURVIVING ARTIFACTS PROVIDE A TANGIBLE HISTORY

The Long Journey Home

The battles of Lexington and Concord, beginning the war for American independence in April 1775, mostly confused and divided those living in the New Jersey colony. Shortly after the Continental Congress declared independence on July 4, 1776, the war came a bit closer to what is present-day West Orange, then part of the Newark settlement. British general Howe invaded nearby Long Island and New York, where the Continental army was defeated, and General George Washington retreated across New Jersey with Howe in close pursuit. This increased the Loyalist sentiment in New Jersey, as the cause for American independence seemed to begin fading away. Then on Christmas Eve 1776, Washington crossed the Delaware River and launched a surprise attack. He won strategic victories at Trenton and Princeton and gained partial control of New Jersey. With renewed confidence, Washington spent the rest of the winter at Morristown, protected behind the hills of the Orange Mountains of the Watchung Mountain Range. But key British outposts remained close by at Newark, Elizabeth and Perth Amboy.

In 1776, living in present-day West Orange were Nathaniel and Mary Williams with their six children. They were married in 1755 and lived in a small farmhouse near the current intersection of Eagle Rock and Harrison Avenues. They were considered well-to-do planters with rich holdings.

Nathaniel's younger brother Benjamin lived in the same area and enjoyed an equally prosperous existence. Both were ingrained with a deep loyalty to the British Crown and remained outspoken about their profound allegiance to England. They frequently met with other Loyalists, called Tories, near the present-day intersection of Washington and Main Streets. This area was originally called Williamsville, but it soon took on the name of Tory Corner, by which it is still known today.

In order for General Washington to take back New Jersey, it meant identifying the Tories and those loyal to the British. In the spring of 1777, Washington ordered local militias throughout New Jersey to find all traitors to the American cause. This order put Nathaniel and Benjamin William in a difficult position. They had been offered protection by the British, but the growing presence of New Jersey militias and surging support for American independence endangered their property holdings and comfortable lifestyles. It was decided that a pardon would be granted to anyone who would change their allegiance to the American cause. The date of August 5, 1777, was set as the deadline by the Council of Public Safety, and as the final hour drew near, Benjamin Williams reluctantly denounced his allegiance to the British and accepted the pardon. He did so not because he believed in American independence but because he was more interested in preserving his wealth and social standing. However, his brother Nathaniel had views more profoundly aligned with the British cause and could not bring himself to side with the American cause.

This issue so deeply divided Nathaniel and his wife, Mary, that he took his two eldest sons, Amos and James, and fled to join the British army in New York City. He left behind his farm and wife and their four youngest children in present-day West Orange. Mary Williams expected to lose the farm and property since it legally belonged to her husband. The law at that time required all land belonging to Tory sympathizers be confiscated and sold at public auction. But Mary petitioned the Council of Public Safety for her family to remain on the farm. She had expressed open disagreement with her husband's beliefs and maintained faith in American independence and was confident in Washington's ultimate victory. Mary could bid only a small fraction for the farm, which was valued at considerably more. Mary was held in such high regard that during the public auction, no one was permitted to bid against her for ownership of the farm. Her outspoken views in favor of independence and her refusal to join her husband in New York with the British had won her favor. No opposing bids were placed at the auction, allowing Mary to keep the farm by being the only bidder.

Mary Williams was considered a true Patriot, despite her family being divided by the issue of American independence. She would never again see her son Amos or her estranged husband, Nathaniel, who died of smallpox in New York in 1782. Before Mary's own death in 1816 at the age of eighty, she welcomed home her other son James, who left with her husband to join the British army. He had been exiled to Nova Scotia for thirty years following the Revolutionary War but eventually returned to Mary for a joyous reunion.

In 1926, a local chapter of the Daughters of the American Revolution officially recognized the struggles and sacrifices of Mary Williams. A bronze tablet was placed on a boulder in front of the Eagle Rock School, now used for West Orange Board of Education offices on Valley Way. The tablet proclaimed:

> *A life consecrated to the cause of American Independence, Mary Williams (1736–1816) maintained her home near this site during the stirring days of the American Revolution, giving freely of her supplies to Washington's troops while her husband Nathaniel, and two sons were with the British forces. Erected in loving memory of this loyal woman by the Mistress Mary Williams Chapter, DAR October 23, 1926.*

It was dedicated to her memory only a stone's throw from the farm where she once lived. However, the bronze tablet was sadly stolen in 1974 and has

Members of the local DAR chapter pose in 1974 in front of the bronze tablet honoring Mary Williams. *Author's collection.*

This house was built by Mary's son Zenas in 1822, replacing the house built circa 1720 by Matthew Williams on the same site, seen here circa 1901. *Author's collection.*

never been replaced. But the boulder proudly remains as a silent testimony and a forgotten memorial to the brave patriotic spirit of a truly heroic and courageous woman.

The one-and-a-half-story farmhouse where Mary Williams lived was built about 1720 by her husband's grandfather Matthew Williams. It was built of quarried stone and was twenty by twenty-eight feet in size. It had a clumsy-looking chimney resembling a stone fence set on end. There was also a roomy garret containing a large grain bin, with a spout at the bottom to draw off the contents, which were protected from the weather. It was a cavernous and gloomy house, with two small windows in the front and an eight-foot-wide entry. It survived to 1822, when it was replaced by a frame structure built by Mary's son Zenas Williams. In 1886, it was purchased by the Bramhall family, and it survived until the early part of the twentieth century, when it was torn down. Today, Our Lady of Lourdes Church now occupies the site of Mary Williams's former home.

In the possession of Nathaniel and Mary Williams at the time of their family's breakup in 1777 over the issue of American independence was a grandfather clock. The brass clockworks bear the name of Stephen Tichenor, an early clock maker located in Newark, New Jersey. When Nathaniel left to join the British in New York City, the clock was given to the safekeeping of his younger brother Benjamin until he returned. When Nathaniel subsequently passed away in 1782, the clock became the property of Benjamin. In the days following the Revolutionary War, Benjamin became locally known as "Governor Ben" because of his large physique and dignified appearance. Although he had taken the pardon offered him in 1777, he had always remained a Tory at heart and contended to the day he died that the Declaration of Independence was a big lie. Although a prominent and prosperous businessman, he pledged to never accept an office within the structure of the new American government. For many years, he attended Trinity Church in Newark, which eventually drew his attention closer to the religious faith of the Church of England. Subsequent meetings at his home led him to organize the founding of St. Mark's Church in West Orange.

When Governor Ben passed away in 1822, his brother Nathaniel's grandfather clock passed to his son Amos. When Amos died in 1843, it went to his son James A. Williams and on to his daughter Selena when James passed away in 1883. Selena F. Williams never married and retained possession of the colonial clock given to her great-grandfather in 1777 until her own death on Friday, August 11, 1922, at the age of eighty. It was from her home at 510 Linden Avenue in Orange, New Jersey, which she had shared with her brother Stephen W. Williams, that the colonial clock, once a treasured family heirloom, vanished.

The old grandfather clock had passed through four generations of the Williams family and had somehow become lost to time after Selena's death. It would have remained that way if not for a note Selena attached to the clock's original cabinet door before it disappeared. In 2008, a curious collector named Doug Raymond spotted that same note with the brass clockworks at a flea market in Bloomington, Illinois. Since the note mentioned a date of 1782, it caught Doug's interest. He negotiated ten dollars off the asking price of fifty dollars and purchased the clockworks, the cabinet door with the note and several other parts belonging to the clock. This note from a typewriter was undated but was signed by Selena F. Williams and listed Nathaniel Williams as the clock's original owner. It also mentioned Tory Corner and St. Mark's Church, both familiar names to West Orange. These clues may have been vague to Doug, but they ultimately would save the clock from permanent obscurity.

Doug had originally purchased the clock as a restoration project that he never got around to completing. He kept it for three years before finally deciding to further investigate the important clues the note offered. By the spring of 2011, he had reached out across the Internet seeking possible answers. His persistent inquiries eventually filtered through to me as a person knowledgeable with West Orange history who might be able to assist him. In our first phone conversation, I knew almost immediately what Doug had stumbled across. I had been aware of the existence of the old grandfather clock once belonging to Nathaniel Williams from previous research on the West Orange colonial period. The Williams family were among the original settlers of West Orange, and the area where they lived was known as Williamsville. The clock is specifically mentioned with their family history in the *Genealogical and Memorial History of the State of New Jersey,* published in 1910. Williamsville eventually took on the name Tory Corner in West Orange, named after Tories, who were those loyal to the British Crown. This was the place where they once gathered, and it is still known by that name today. I offered to buy the clock from Doug, but sharing the story seemed to renew his interest, and he decided to keep the clockworks as an interesting old colonial timepiece.

I subsequently remained in touch with Doug by e-mail and often inquired about the Williams family clock. He was always very cordial and polite, with prompt responses to my periodic inquiries. My intention was to keep track of the clock with the hope that one day he might consider selling it to me. Finally, in January 2014, perhaps realizing it was time to let it go, Doug offered to sell me the clock. His asking price was considerably more than he paid and more consistent with the price of colonial timepieces. Despite the cost, I saw this as a genuine priceless West Orange artifact with nearly 264 years of amazing history. I reached out to the West Orange community, and several generous people came forward with donations helping to offset the cost and allowing me to make the purchase. The clock has now made the long journey back home to West Orange where it rightfully belongs. It will hardly recognize the place it knew in 1777 before beginning an extraordinary pilgrimage through the centuries spanning four generations. The exact circumstances surrounding its disappearance and ensuing eighty-six-year exile in oblivion remain a mystery hopefully to be solved one day. It now endures as a tangible piece of local history rescued from the bottomless abyss of obscurity. It survives as a timeless memorial to the courage and patriotic spirit of Mary Williams, who once cast her eyes on it. I will vigilantly endeavor to be a worthy steward as it continues on an incredible passage through time.

John Crosby Brown

One of West Orange's most generous and prominent residents was the New York City banker John Crosby Brown. The company founded by his grandfather still survives today as Brown Brothers and Harriman. Brown first acquired a forty-acre wooded tract along the ridge in West Orange in the mid-1870s. It was here that he would clear the land and build his permanent summer home named Brighthurst as part of a sprawling estate and became a neighbor to General George McClellan.

John Crosby Brown passed away at Brighthurst on June 24, 1909. In 1925, a fire destroyed many of the outbuildings on Brown's former estate. The house

John Crosby Brown, seen shortly before his death in 1909. *Author's collection.*

was spared but was torn down a few years later when the property was sold in 1928 to Edwin Greble Jr. The former carriage house spared in the fire was eventually sold in 1950 to the West Orange Women's Club. Today, it is the site of the Shillelagh Club on Prospect Avenue, and even though it has undergone renovations, it is perhaps the only surviving building from Brown's time. The club's present driveway was once a cow path used by Brown for cattle coming from pasture on what is now the Essex County Country Club. The remaining grounds of the former Brown estate eventually became property of the former Carteret School and today are part of the athletic fields of Seton Hall Preparatory School on Prospect Avenue. John Crosby Brown has left his mark on West Orange history in many ways that are not often viewed or understood in the proper historical context.

Perhaps the most visible surviving artifact left behind by Brown is what's known as the Pilgrim Cross. It was a memorial erected in 1878 by Brown to the early settlers who had traveled on a path known as the Christian Path. This old route passing over the first Orange Mountain was originally used by Indians before the early settlers. It was nothing more then a path through the forest that was gradually widened by continuous use probably beginning as early as 1720. By the mid-nineteenth century, the path had been used for years as a shortcut by worshipers traveling from outlying districts throughout western Essex County. They came by foot, with some walking from as far away as Caldwell, then known as Horse Neck. Their intent was to attend worship services at the meetinghouse in Orange, which was the forerunner of the First Presbyterian Church of Orange, while others continued on to St. John's in Newark. It was for this reason that the route eventually took on the name of the Christian Path.

The route it followed came up Old Indian Road toward Prospect Avenue. At that time, it was known only as Mountain Avenue and provided a narrow winding route up the mountain to connect with Prospect Avenue. As the name suggests, Old Indian Road actually once was part of an old Indian trail. Even today, travel along one section of Old Indian Road can be a bit rugged. As it made its way past the intersection opposite Ridgeway Avenue, it passed by what could be the oldest house in West Orange, which dates to about 1740. Many of the early travelers using the path would have known this exact house and property. Here the route passed by the St. Cloud Presbyterian Church, now the United Presbyterian Church of West Orange. It crossed Prospect Avenue and continued straight up what is essentially now the driveway of 670 Prospect Avenue. Today, one of two original stone pillars marking the rear entrance to the Browns' former home, Brighthurst, can still be seen. The Christian Path crossed Brown's property at the top of the mountain at Ridge Road and headed down the steep mountainside. It entered Northfield Avenue below the old quarry at what was known as Bluebirds Bend, now the site of the small Ron Jolyn Apartment complex. Legend has it that in order to save shoe leather, the trip was often made barefooted until reaching Northfield Avenue on the final approach to Orange.

When John Crosby Brown realized the Christian Path crossed his property, he constructed a stone cross in 1878 as a remembrance to those who passed along the route. The stone cross was quarried from the same mountainside where it originally sat just below Ridge Road and became known as the Pilgrim Cross. When John Crosby Brown passed away in 1909, John Schroll, a florist, purchased the land where the stone cross was located between Northfield Avenue and Ridge Road from the Brown estate. Sometime during the 1930s, the cross was damaged when it fell over in a storm. It was cemented back together by John Schroll and William Robertson, who was the gardener for the Delano family, a neighbor to Schroll. When John Schroll passed away, his son Ditlow moved the cross to his home in St. Cloud.

The Pilgrim Cross at its present location remains just as it would have looked to countless travelers along the Christian Path. *Author's collection.*

Several years later, Ditlow decided to move the cross closer to the original Christian Path, where it now sits at the entrance to the United Presbyterian Church of West Orange. Here, the Pilgrim Cross can still be seen, with the inscription on the original stone plaque at the base of the cross bearing the year 1878 and the words: "The Christian pilgrims, who this pathway trod, are now in Heaven and walk with God."

If not for John Crosby Brown's generosity, we might not know the Christian Path story today. Coincidentally, the church entrance where the cross now stands was originally the St. Cloud Presbyterian Church, which Brown helped found in 1877.

The eastern edge of John Crosby Brown's property was bordered along the ridge by the Spottiswoode Quarry on Northfield Avenue. When John Crosby Brown realized that quarrymen were blasting away the most beautiful part of the mountain, he decided something must be done. Brown summoned the owner of the quarry to his home and requested a selling price for the property. A deal was made, and John Crosby Brown reportedly paid over $50,000 to preserve the mountain ridge in the late 1890s.

With operations in the quarry brought to a halt by Brown's land purchase, his property now stretched from Prospect Avenue to Northfield Avenue. In about 1900, he constructed a springhouse for weary travelers at the site of the former quarry. It was a small wooden structure over a watering hole on his property bordering Northfield Avenue. An iron plaque at the base of the springhouse read: "Stay weary traveler rest awhile, no banquet this nor merry feast. But here will flow at thy desire pure water for both man and beast."

The springhouse of John Crosby Brown has now given away to modern development and is long gone. But amazingly, at the site of the former springhouse, the same iron plaque still exists sitting between two homes on the north side of Northfield Avenue, just slightly below Prospect Avenue.

Today's weary travelers and daily commuters now zip past the former location on present-day Northfield Avenue, perhaps not worrying about a drink of water. But in another time and era, this West Orange location was an important resting place where fresh spring water could be had. It still bears witness to the forgotten memory and far-reaching benevolence of John Crosby Brown.

John Crosby Brown's well house on March 19, 1903. The cliffs of the former quarry can be seen in the background. *Author's collection.*

Brown's daughter Mary Magoun Brown graduated from the Presbyterian Hospital Nursing School in New York City in 1897. Shortly after, Brown was influenced by his wife and daughter, who explained to him that nurses in New York City needed reprieves from their hectic and often demanding work to a refreshing country setting in the Orange Mountains of West Orange. Brown was quick to recognize this need and, in 1907, established the Brownery, located at 18 Fairview Avenue in West Orange. It was a convalescent and rest home for nurses only a short distance from Brown's Brighthurst home. The Brownery operated under the direction of Miss Claxon and offered rooms on the second and third floors at the cost of five dollars per week. After John Crosby Brown passed away in 1909, the Brownery continued to operate until 1914. It was then relocated to Nyack-on-the-Hudson, New York, under the new name of the New Haven Country Club. Today, the former Brownery in West Orange is still standing as a private residence neatly tucked away in a quiet St. Cloud neighborhood whose memory has all but faded into history.

Mrs. Edison and Mrs. Roosevelt

The names of Thomas Edison and Theodore Roosevelt are likely familiar to most schoolchildren. Perhaps lesser known are the women who played important roles in both of their husbands' careers. The only time Mrs. Edison and Mrs. Roosevelt crossed paths was a historic meeting for both women in West Orange.

Thomas Edison endures as the most iconic image of West Orange, but he was practically world famous before ever coming to town. He invented the phonograph in 1877 and was credited with perfecting the electric light bulb in 1879 in Menlo Park, New Jersey. It was there that he married his first wife, Mary Stilwell, in 1871. However, she sadly passed away only thirteen years later in 1884 from an extended illness. A subsequent fire destroyed Edison's Menlo Park facility, and he was looking to rebuild at a new location. On February 24, 1886, Edison remarried twenty-one-year-old Mina Miller. Edison gave her the choice of living in the city or the country. Mina preferred the country, so Edison purchased the Llewellyn Park home named Glenmont in West Orange, which was considered the country at that time, fully furnished as her wedding gift. The following year, in 1887, Edison built his new laboratories on the corner of Main Street and Lakeside

Avenue. Today, both his laboratories and former home survive in West Orange as museums of the Thomas Edison National Historical Park, run by the National Park Service.

Unlike his first wife, Mary, who was frequently sick, Edison's second wife, Mina, was a more active woman. She often devoted her time to community groups, social functions and charities, as well as trying to improve her husband's social and personal habits. She was regularly seen driving around town and even once gave my father and his friend Ken Tinquist a ride in Edison's electric car as curious youngsters growing up in West Orange. Thomas Edison died in 1931, and Mina remarried a few years later in 1935 to her childhood friend Edward Everett Hughes. Mina Edison then became Mrs. Hughes, and the couple lived at Glenmont. Edward Hughes passed away on January 19, 1940, and during the time of her marriage to Hughes, she often continued using her Edison surname, being known as Mrs. Mina Edison Hughes.

Like Mary Edison, the first wife of Theodore Roosevelt also passed away. Theodore Roosevelt had married Alice Hathaway Lee in 1880. However, four years later, in 1884, both Alice and Roosevelt's mother died in the same house on the same day. The immediate aftermath of this double tragedy plunged Theodore Roosevelt into a deep depression. He interrupted his career and embarked on a journey of self-discovery to the Dakota Territory. There he spent time as a ranch hand and deputy sheriff and would ultimately emerge as a renewed man with a rekindled spirit.

Theodore Roosevelt's sister Corinne Roosevelt married Douglas Robinson Jr. in 1882, and they made their home in West Orange from 1894 to 1911. Corinne was a playmate and childhood friend of Edith Kermit Carow, who Theodore also knew very well. Edith was even an invited guest at the 1880 wedding of Theodore Roosevelt and Alice Hathaway Lee. Five years after the death of his first wife, Roosevelt became reacquainted with Edith, and a romance soon blossomed with his sister's friend. Theodore Roosevelt remarried his sister's friend Edith Kermit Carow on December 2, 1886. She became first lady of the United States in 1901 when President McKinley was assassinated and Vice President Theodore Roosevelt became the twenty-fifth president. Roosevelt eventually won a second term and served as president of the United States until 1909. He passed away in 1919.

In 1940, both Mrs. Mina Edison Hughes and Edith K. Roosevelt met in West Orange for the first and only time in history. The meeting occurred at the new Carteret School, which had opened on Prospect Avenue earlier that year. The school first opened in 1901 in Orange, New Jersey, as the Carteret

Left to right: Lawrence Norton, Mrs. Edith K. Roosevelt, George Hofe, Mrs. Mina M. Edison Hughes and Bradford Palmer on May 9, 1940. *Author's collection.*

The Carteret School handbook signed by both Mrs. Roosevelt and Mrs. Edison. *Author's collection.*

Academy but changed its name to the Carteret School when it moved to West Orange.

An awards ceremony held at the new school on May 9, 1940, featured both Mrs. Edison Hughes and Mrs. Roosevelt as presenters of the Edison and Roosevelt Awards, issued by the school and so named in honor of their respective husbands. The awards were presented to students Lawrence Norton and Bradford Palmer, who were awarded and chosen for outstanding thoroughness, accuracy, perseverance and practicability, which the school felt was also characteristic of both Thomas Edison and Theodore Roosevelt. Following the Carteret School presentation, a luncheon was held at the South Orange home of the school's president, George Hofe. It was there that a Carteret School handbook was autographed by both women to commemorate the occasion. The back cover was also signed by about a dozen invited guests to the luncheon. The awards ceremony occurred only four months after the death of Mina Edison's second husband, Edward, and she signed her name using both the Edison and Hughes surnames.

Mina Edison Hughes died at age eighty-two in 1947 at the Columbia-Presbyterian Medical Center in New York City. Edith Kermit Carow Roosevelt died at age eighty-seven in 1948 in her Oyster Bay home in New York. The Carteret School handbook they signed in West Orange is perhaps the only document bearing the autograph of both these two distinguished women of American history.

Chapter 2

KEY ROLES OF TRANSPORTATION

The Eagle Rock Hill Climb

Motorists traveling up present-day Eagle Rock Avenue in West Orange are mostly oblivious to the historic nature of their otherwise uneventful and brief journey. However, more than a century ago, this small town helped play a small but vital role in the development of the automobile.

In 1900, the first ever New York City auto show was held at Madison Square Garden and introduced the world to the future potential of the new horseless carriage. Although still in its infancy, a wide variety of ideas were all being experimented with as motive power for the emerging technology. Gasoline and steam-driven engines, as well as electric vehicles, were all being developed. The steep grade and sharp turns on Eagle Rock Avenue made it the perfect venue by which the mechanical capabilities of these machines could be tested and challenged.

Prior to the advent of the automobile, Eagle Rock Avenue was used by bicycling enthusiasts for hill climbing events dating until at least 1888. The first bicycle club in New Jersey was the Essex Bicycle Club and was only the third such club in the United States. It was founded in West Orange on March 8, 1879, with Llewellyn H. Johnson as team captain. The first headquarters for the new club was located at the home of Johnson's father, just a short distance off Eagle Rock Avenue. The steep hill presented a natural setting for cyclists to challenge themselves and train for endurance. By May 1879,

White tape seen stretched across the bottom of Eagle Rock Avenue on November 24, 1904, marks the staring line. *Author's collection.*

the club moved its headquarters to Broad Street in Newark but continued using Eagle Rock Avenue for hill climb events and competitions with other bicycle clubs.

On November 5, 1901, the Automobile Club of New Jersey, also located in Newark, sponsored the first Eagle Rock Hill Climb in West Orange. The club likely chose to come to West Orange because it was aware that cyclists had been successfully using Eagle Rock Avenue for years. Automotive hill climbs had recently become popular in Europe and were still new to the United States, so in 1901, this event was the first ever in New Jersey and one of the first in the country. Drivers would not directly race one another up the hill as in a traditional race but would be competing for the best time against the clock in their specific classification of automobile. The course began at the bottom of present-day Eagle Rock Avenue and Main Street.

They were allowed a flying start down Harrison Avenue prior to the starting point in front of the present Our Lady of Lourdes Church. Drivers continued up Eagle Rock Avenue, with a sharp left turn to the finish line inside the Eagle Rock Reservation. It wasn't until 1957 when the current road alignment and entrance to Eagle Rock were changed to reflect where they are today.

Shortly after 2:00 p.m. on November 5, 1901, Kirk Brown, the official starter for the first Eagle Rock Hill Climb, stretched a white tape across Eagle Rock Avenue just north of Harrison Avenue. Brown shouted, "Number 1 car in position!"

W.R. Royce, the first participant, pulled up to the tape marking the starting line in a small four-wheeled car, ready and anxious to go. Starter Brown informed Mr. Royce that if his car was disabled before reaching the first turn to the right, he was to pull off the course and keep to the left. He also told Royce that if he was not ready, he could withdraw. Royce acknowledged that he was ready with a confident nod. Starter Brown then began the countdown and gave the signal as he shouted, "Go!" W.R. Royce became the first to ascend the steep grade in West Orange at the first Eagle Rock Hill Climb as he rode up the hill, blazing a dusty trail into history. One by one, each of the remaining participants took his turn at the starting line as they also made history at one of the very first automotive hill climbs in the country. Modern-day auto racing as we know it eventually evolved from this earliest form of competitions known as hill climbs.

Most of the participants in 1901 lacked sufficient power and couldn't complete the climb. However, two of the drivers who reached the top set world records in the process. Most notably is Charles E. Duryea, of Springfield, Massachusetts, who is credited with inventing the first gasoline-powered buggy in the United States in 1892. Duryea came to West Orange and won in the gasoline engine category, setting a record of three minutes and forty-five seconds. The fastest overall time was turned in by W.J. Steward of Newark in the steam engine category in his Locomobile Steamer in an amazing two minutes and forty-three seconds.

The Eagle Rock Hill Climb of 1901 intended to become an annual event when most traffic was still horse and buggy. It was subsequently held in West Orange in 1902, 1903 and 1904. The West Orange event had quickly grown from only a few spectators and thirteen participants in 1901 to a crowd of nearly three thousand and thirty-six drivers by 1903. Most notable among the drivers was Willie K. Vanderbilt, great-grandson of wealthy railroad tycoon Cornelius Vanderbilt. Vanderbilt had set a world record in West Orange in 1903 for the fastest time up Eagle Rock Avenue at one minute and thirty-four seconds. Perhaps inspired by his victory in West Orange, Vanderbilt returned home to Long Island, where in October 1904, he inaugurated the Vanderbilt Cup Races. They were the first international road races in the United States and were subsequently held annually until 1910.

Harlan Whipple of East Orange participated with his eleven-year-old son, Harold, in the 1903 Eagle Rock Hill Climb. *Author's collection.*

In 1903, the entries for the class of electrical cars included Harold Whipple. He was the son of Harlan Whipple, who finished in third place behind Vanderbilt that year in the gasoline engine class. However, his son Harold was only eleven years old and completed the course in 7:39½ driving a five-horsepower National Electric runabout. Harold Whipple finished in second place and was beaten by a more powerful eight-horsepower Columbia Electric owned by Thomas Edison's New York Edison Company.

Edison himself was on hand that day to witness eleven-year-old Harold Whipple's defeat by his Columbia electric car. But perhaps Whipple scored an even greater victory. He will go down in history as the youngest person to ever legally drive an automobile up Eagle Rock Avenue in West Orange in a day when no driver's license was required.

Vanderbilt returned to West Orange in 1904 but faced a far fiercer competitor in a growing rivalry. Also from Long Island and sharing similar interests in racing automobiles with Vanderbilt was William Gould Brokaw. *The Great Gatsby*, written by F. Scott Fitzgerald, focused on the fictional character of a prosperous millionaire named Jay Gatsby living in 1922 Long Island. It has often been suggested that William Gould Brokaw may have been the inspiration for Fitzgerald's 1925 novel. Brokaw had participated in the first Vanderbilt Cup Race of 1904 in Long Island against Vanderbilt. But his powerful Renault, driven by Maurice Bernin of France in that race, finished in a disappointing seventeenth place due to mechanical difficulties.

Following the Vanderbilt Cup Race on Long Island, both Vanderbilt and Brokaw returned to West Orange to face off once again in the 1904 Eagle Rock Hill Climb. Brokaw had made the necessary repairs to his Renault and was poised to challenge Vanderbilt's world record set on

Brokaw's sixty-horsepower Renault, driven by Maurice Bernin, crosses the finish line at Eagle Rock on November 24, 1904, setting a new world record. *Author's collection.*

Willie K. Vanderbilt, in his ninety-horsepower Mercedes used at Eagle Rock in 1904, is seen at Ormond, Florida, in 1905. *Author's collection.*

Eagle Rock Avenue the previous year. Vanderbilt came to West Orange with a more powerful car than he had used the previous year. He had replaced his thirty-horsepower Mors car with a ninety-horsepower Mercedes, intent on beating Brokaw's car. The driver of Brokaw's sixty-horsepower Renault was once again the Frenchman Maurice Bernin. On November 24, 1904, Bernin, driving Brokaw's car, beat Vanderbilt's 1903 record and set a new world record of one minute and twenty seconds. Bernin also beat rival Vanderbilt's bigger and more powerful ninety-horsepower Mercedes by only three-fifths of a second.

The event was witnessed by an estimated crowd of five thousand spectators lining the route along Eagle Rock Avenue and often dangerously wandering onto the course. This really caught the attention of West Orange town officials, and although an event was planned for 1905, it was deemed too dangerous and subsequently was canceled. An attempt was made in 1910 to resume the event, but it failed to gain support, and permits—which now became necessary—were denied.

To commemorate the fiftieth anniversary of the first Eagle Rock Hill Climb, a nostalgic comeback was made on Saturday, November 3, 1951, up the Eagle Rock Avenue course. Cars similar to the ones first used participated in the event, which was sponsored by the Automobile Club of New Jersey. Unfortunately, the weather didn't cooperate, and the Eagle Rock Hill Climb Golden Jubilee was held in a driving snowstorm. About thirty antique cars participated in the competition followed by a parade through West Orange to the parking lot of the Edison Museum. A luncheon, with ceremonies marking the event, was held afterward at Mayfair Farms hosted by Mayor Degnan of West Orange. The many distinguished guests included M.J. Duryea, whose father, Charles E. Duryea, was the inventor of the gasoline-powered buggy and who participated in 1901. Also in attendance were former New Jersey governor Charles A. Edison, son of Thomas Edison and Theodore T. Maxfield, who were both present at the first Eagle Rock Hill Climb fifty years earlier. Anniversary Eagle Rock Hill Climbs were subsequently held in 1956 and 1976. They were only ceremonial and nothing more than the equivalent of a parade for antique cars up Eagle Rock Avenue.

The evolution of the early automobile certainly was on a collision course with destiny before ever coming to West Orange. But often lost to history is the important role Eagle Rock Avenue once played as the road of development passed through West Orange.

Moving a Mountain

Traveling east along I-280, motorists enter the physical boundaries of West Orange by mile marker 7 just before approaching the interchange of Pleasant Valley Way. However, you ride over sections of West Orange about five miles before actually entering town in East Hanover in Morris County.

Just before crossing the Passaic River into Essex County, the highway passes through the wetlands of the Hatfield Swamp. Here the roadbed for I-280 was raised and filled in with excavated rock mostly taken from West Orange during construction.

The genesis of 280 actually began in 1939, when the concept for today's national interstate highway system was first reported to Congress. Ten years later, the William A. Stickel Memorial Bridge over the Passaic River opened in 1949. The new bridge was part of the Essex Freeway, which was a 1.1-mile highway named Route 25A connecting Harrison to Newark. In 1953, a small western extension was added, and it was redesigned as NJ Route 58. In 1956, the Eisenhower administration provided for funding and building of an interstate highway system. The federal government plan proposed an interstate in New Jersey along the previously constructed Route 3 corridor. The New Jersey State Highway Department objected, stating that it did not meet interstate standards and could not be economically modified to conform. A new route was then selected that would expand on the existing Essex Freeway, renamed the East–West Freeway and given the official designation of Interstate I-280 in 1957.

The new east–west corridor set its sites on expanding west from Newark, but East Orange, Orange and the mountains of West Orange stood directly in its path. The objective was a connection to Interstate 80 in Parsippany, which was a planned transcontinental interstate route connecting New York City with San Francisco, California. An overly optimistic completion date of 1961 was originally planned for I-280, but an astonishing number of unforeseen setbacks caused delays. By July 1963, only one mile of the new freeway was opened, and work was just beginning on an additional one and a half miles of the original nearly fifteen-mile route. A lawsuit filed by East Orange fought plans for an elevated highway and won a decision against NJDOT, forcing the highway to be depressed through the city rather then be built overhead.

The town of West Orange also waged its own fight against the NJDOT in its plans to build the highway through an open rock cut on the first and second mountains. An effort spearheaded by then West Orange mayor James Sheeren sought to have the highway tunneled through the first mountain near Prospect Avenue. Sheeran wanted to retain the land rights above the tunnel for West Orange taxpayers, and Sheeran also saw the tunnel being possibly used as a bomb shelter during the height of the Cold War.

The proposal was defeated, and plans for an open rock cut at a 6 percent grade moved forward. However, in 1966, the entire freeway project was dealt

S.J. Groves train in the deep rock cut of the first mountain waiting to be loaded on April 9, 1971. *Author's collection.*

a financial setback when the U.S. Congress approved funding for highway construction that did not include money for I-280. Construction halted, and the completed unused sections of the highway soon became dangerous eyesores. A feeling of bitterness developed since land taken for the construction of the freeway now went unused. Orange, East Orange and West Orange had considered a joint legal action against the state to recover lost tax ratables while the completed road sections remained closed and unused.

By 1970, after nearly four years of sitting idle, new funding had been approved. New Jersey officials were prepared to give the freeway construction top priority, but still no date was set for opening. In June 1972, a key section between the Garden State Parkway in East Orange and Newark eventually opened. In the fall of 1972, I-280 finally reached West Orange when two additional miles were opened to Northfield Avenue.

The deep one-hundred-foot rock cut through the first mountain in West Orange was also now continuing at breakneck speed. The contractor for this section of highway was S.J. Groves & Sons, a Minneapolis-based contractor.

The construction for I-280 was undertaken by various contractors, each responsible for a different section of roadway. In 1969, S.J. Groves was awarded the contract for a Morris County section. Between the two sections was a stretch of graded but unpaved roadway being completed by a different contractor. It was estimated that 1.5 million cubic yards of rock and dirt would need to be removed to clear the route through the mountain in West Orange. Coincidentally, the Morris County section, which began six miles away, needed almost an equal amount of fill to raise the roadbed. The obvious way to solve the problem was to move the West Orange rock to Morris County. Not so obvious was the means by which it would be accomplished.

Most highway contractors would have considered a fleet of dump trucks. It was determined that about thirty to fifty trucks would be needed. However, the costs were staggering considering the trucks would have to run day and night. The sobering task had to be completed before the end of 1971. The entire fleet of trucks would need to replace tires every couple weeks because of the heavy loads. This, combined with other operating costs, would have sent expenses through the roof. A feasibility study conducted by the McDowell-Wellman Company of Cleveland found a solution.

It was determined that a temporary railroad between the Essex County section and the Morris County section was the most economical answer. The study by McDowell-Wellman indicated that twenty-four specially designed side-dump cars with a thirty-five-cubic-yard capacity could handle the job. These cars would be divided into three trains of eight cars each. The plan was to have one train in the loading zone, one train in the dump zone and one train in transit at all times.

The temporary railroad was constructed by the Railcon Corporation of Plainfield, New Jersey, using panels of prefabricated rail, thirty-three feet long each. The rail sections were delivered by flatbed truck and hoisted into position by crane. The trains were pulled by two General Electric U33 diesel locomotives built new for S.J. Groves.

They arrived in November 1969 from Binghamton, New York, over a rail connection made to the Morristown and Erie Railroad in Roseland. The initial length of the railroad was approximately six miles long with sidings enabling east–west trains to pass one another. Eventually, the line extended more than eleven and a half miles as progress moved westward. Interestingly, the locomotives were run by members of Operating Engineers Local 825, not experienced railroad men. The completed rock cut is now used by thousands of motorists who pass through it daily, perhaps unaware that a mountain was once hauled away by train on the same roadbed now used for

Seen in the West Orange rock cut is one of two GE U33 locomotives built for S.J. Groves in 1969. *Author's collection.*

travel and commerce. Four million cubic yards of excavated West Orange rock was hauled away as fill for the western sections in Morris County.

Finally, after ten years of construction, twenty-five years of planning and $186 million in expenses, the East–West Freeway, better known as I-280, opened end to end on Friday, June 22, 1973. Today, a seventeen-mile interstate highway connects the New Jersey Turnpike with Interstate 80. The Orange Mountains proved to be no obstacle for an interstate highway that now permanently defines the landscape of modern-day West Orange.

The Cable Road

Over a century ago, a business venture rooted in land speculation spawned the original idea of the Cable Road. It was conceived by Edward A. Pearson, along with his two partners, Francis Eppley and Thomas Marsh, with Pearson the driving force behind the group. The main focus of Pearson's vision was not really rooted in transportation but rather land speculation. His idea was to develop the land on top of the Orange Mountains above the Orange Valley in West Orange. He realized that in order to do so, a reliable means of transportation to the proposed homesites was necessary. The closest road was Northfield Avenue, but the grade and curves were both steep and dangerous for regular and safe passage. Pearson understood that once all the land was sold, the land company would dissolve. But the so-called genius of his plan was that he optimistically thought cable cars could then serve as a perpetual means for transportation up the mountain. He felt he could successfully purchase the land, sell the home sites, dissolve the land company, and forever provide the transportation to the land he developed by means of the Cable Road.

Pearson and his partners formed two affiliated companies: the Orange Mountain Cable Company and the Orange Mountain Land Company. Early maps show the vast amounts of land purchased and owned in the St. Cloud area of West Orange by the Orange Mountain Land Company. Pearson and company began construction on the Cable Road in 1887. But as the project neared completion, they ran into trouble as their financial resources were apparently stretched too thin. George Spottiswood, a contractor hired by Pearson to construct the Cable Road, hadn't been paid. As a result, nearly all the land owned by the Orange Mountain Land Company, including the nearly completed Cable Road, came into possession of George Spottiswood to satisfy the debt.

Finally, by the summer of 1892, the Cable Road, under the ownership of George Spottiswood and his associates, began operations. They also remained hopeful about selling the home sites of the Orange Mountain Land Company, just as Edward Pearson had envisioned.

The Cable Road of the Orange Mountain Cable Company used two specially constructed cable cars on two tracks. A continuous cable connected both on a large drum to a powerhouse at the top of the mountain. When one car was pulled up, the other was automatically lowered, acting as a counterweight. The engineer in the powerhouse had a clear line of sight down the entire route, and he could be signaled by the conductor on board the cable cars to safely raise and lower both cars as needed. Each car had a large open platform that could accommodate passengers, bicycles, cargo and even an entire team of horses.

However, after a few years of operations, the Orange Mountain Cable Company, under the ownership of George Spottiswood, again found itself in financial trouble. Patronage was more as a curiosity than as a practical means of transportation. This, combined with sluggish land sales on the mountain, forced it to close in 1895. After only three short years of operation

One of the specially designed cable cars of the cable road is seen ascending the mountain circa 1892. *Courtesy Ted Gleichmann Jr.*

that took nearly five years of backbreaking construction, the Cable Road faced an uncertain future.

By 1898, George Spottiswood reorganized the Orange Mountain Cable Company under the name of the Orange Mountain Traction Company, and operations resumed. There was renewed optimism in success because an amusement park named Highland Park was constructed at the top of the mountain, serving as a destination to attract customers. It also featured picnic grounds with a large pavilion and dance hall and refreshment stands. A small natural lake near Highland Park was enlarged and named Cable Lake. Today, it still remains in the shadow of the present-day clubhouse on the grounds of the Rock Spring Country Club in West Orange. This golf course is part of the former location of many of the planned home sites of the Orange Mountain Land Company. The lake provided fishing, and in the winter months, it was possible to ice skate on the lake while enjoying music from the nearby dance hall pavilion. An ornamental iron pedestrian bridge was also constructed across the deep rock cut at this time that became the centerpiece of the new park. The bridge offered a breathtaking and spectacular view of the Orange Valley as never seen before.

The abandoned pedestrian bridge leading to the picnic grounds stirs curiosity for an unidentified group of West Orange boys circa 1910. *Author's collection.*

It was truly the golden age of the Cable Road, but despite its increased popularity, it was still plagued by financial troubles. The West Orange cable car era soon ended for good when service was terminated in 1902, and the Cable Road ceased operations forever. The vision of the Cable Road of Edward Pearson and subsequent owner George Spottiswood was unfortunately never fully realized.

The Orange Mountain Traction Company ultimately decided that no profit existed in operating a cable railroad. It shifted focus on converting to the emerging technology of the day with trolleys powered by overhead wires. Advances in electricity and powerful traction motors seemed to hold more promise. It also offered the possibility of attracting more customers by becoming part of an expanding network. Trolleys were more versatile and could reach areas cable cars could not. Finally, by 1906, after laying new rails and running overhead wires, the company was ready to resume operations by running trolleys straight up the mountain over the steep route of the former Cable Road.

Some questions were raised that the steepest part of the grade near the top might not be suited for trolleys. These concerns were alleviated by company officials stating that the trolley cars were outfitted with a newly patented

safety braking system. Also, an auxiliary cable would be attached to the cars as an added safety precaution once they crossed Gregory Avenue before entering the steepest part of the grade. This cable would not provide any pulling power but could catch the cars in the event of brake failure.

The two new trolley cars of the Orange Mountain Traction Company were numbered 101 and 102. Company officials planned to test the new trolley on its first run before the line would be opened to the public. On Sunday morning, June 24, 1906, car 102 began the inaugural run up the

The scene at the bottom of Valley Road following the crash of runaway car 102 on June 24, 1906. *Courtesy Frank Seifiert III.*

mountain. Everything seemed to be working fine as it approached Gregory Avenue without incident. At this location, the car was to stop briefly so that the auxiliary cable could be attached. However, the motorman decided to ignore this safety measure since the car was rolling along swiftly and gaining momentum. It entered the steepest part of the grade without the auxiliary cable and relied solely on the power of the traction motors and the new braking system. As it approached the big rock cut, the grade got steeper and the wheels started to slip. The new brakes were applied and gripped the car to the rails as designed. However, as the car came to a dead stop with a jerk, it almost threw the motorman off his feet. His lurching body released the brake lever, and car 102 began rolling back down the hill out of control. One person jumped off at Gregory Avenue and was killed. Car 102 crashed into car 101 parked at the bottom, hurling it airborne across Valley Road.

It landed in an empty lot alongside D'Alessandro's Hotel on Valley Road. This building is still standing as the present-day Suzy Q's Restaurant. Both cars were completely destroyed and several other people were injured. On the first day of operations, the new line was forced to close. The idea of trolleys ascending straight up the steep grade was quickly abandoned.

Two years later, a safer route using switchbacks from the Orange Valley up the mountain was constructed, crossing the route of the old cable road several times. The line was extended to Northfield Avenue and terminated by the Rock Spring Water Company. The name Mountain Railway Company was used, and most pictures show it painted on the side of the trolley cars. A 1914 trolley guide, however, lists the line leased from the Orange Mountain

A rare view showing Orange Mountain and not Mountain Railway Company painted on the side of the trolley is seen on Northfield Avenue circa 1914. *Author's collection.*

Mountain Railway Time Table

SUMMER SERVICE

Sundays, extra trips, see card in waiting rooms.

SUBJECT TO CHANGE WITHOUT NOTICE

At the End of This Car Line
ROCK SPRING INN
"That Little Country Tea House"

Where one can have a real home luncheon, dinner or afternoon tea, amidst the quaintest and prettiest of surroundings. Picnic and automobile luncheons prepared. Orders taken for home use. Just phone us. Orange 1896-J

DRINK ROCK SPRING WATER

Leave Hoboken	Arrive Highland Ave. Station	Leave Christopher St. Mountain Ry.	Arrive Gregory Ave.	Arrive Cable Lake	Arrive St. Cloud	Arrive Rock Spring	Leave Rock Spring	Arrive St. Cloud	Arrive Cable Lake	Arrive Gregory Ave.	Arrive Christopher St.	Leave Highland Ave. Station	Arrive Hoboken
A.M.							**A.M.**						
6.30	7.06	7.22	7.26	7.30	7.35			7.35	7.39	7.43	7.47	8.00	8.28
6.45	7.19	8.08	8.12	8.16	8.20	8.22	8.25	8.27	8.31	8.35	8.39	8.55	9.24
8.20	8.53	9.08	9.12	9.16	9.20	9.22	9.35	9.37	9.41	9.45	9.49	10.08	10.45
9.30	10.02	10.10	10.14	10.18	10.22	10.24	10.35	10.37	10.41	10.45	10.49	11.06	11.40
9.45	10.20	11.08	11.12	11.16	11.20	11.22	11.35	11 37	11.41	11.45	11.49	12.15	12 45
11.02	11.34	12.08	12.12	12.16	12.20	12.22	**P.M**	12.50	12.52	12.56	1.00	1.04	1.22	1.52
P.M.													
12.28	12.59	1.08	1.12	1.16	1.20	1.22	1.30	1.32	1.36	1.40	1.44	2.00	2.35
												2.40	3.12
1.03	1.33	2.08	2.12	2.15	2.18	2.20	2.20	2.22	2.26	2.30	2.34	3.20	3.50
1.50	2.24	2.38	2.42	2.46	2.50	2.52	3.00	3.02	3.06	3.10	3.14	3.42	4.12
2.23	2.55	3.23	3.27	3.31	3.35	3.37	3.40	3.42	3.46	3.50	3.54	4.20	4.55
3.15	3.50	4.08	4.12	4.15	4.18	4.20	4.20	4.22	4.26	4.30	4.34	4.50	5.26
3.50	4.23	4.38	4.42	4.46	4.50	4.52	5.00	5.02	5.06	5.10	5.14	5.40	6.12
4.30	5.02	5.23	5.27	5.31	5.35	5.37	5.40	5.42	5.46	5.50	5.54	6.15	6.47
5.15	5.53	6.08	6.12	6.15	6.18	6.20	6.20	6.22	6.26	6.30	6.34	6.40	7.18
5.45	6.21	6.38	6.42	6.45	6.48	6.50	6.50	6.52	6.56	7.00	7.04	7.11	7.42
6.25	6.55	7.10	7.13	7.16	7.18	7.20	7.20	7.22	7.26	7.30	7.34	8.03	8.34

This timetable circa 1910 features ads for the Rock Spring Inn and Bungalow Sites for the proposed Orange Mountain Park development, which never succeeded. *Author's collection.*

Traction Company to the Mountain Railway Company. The line operated from 1908 to 1914 and forever brought to a close an important chapter of local transportation history and, by extension, the once glamorous cable cars of West Orange.

The Eagle Rock Trolley

Enjoying the breathtaking view at Eagle Rock has been popular for generations. Despite abundant natural beauty, the rugged terrain made Eagle Rock mostly only reachable by foot or horseback. By the late 1870s, Eagle Rock began to develop as a resort, and a growing need for public transportation eventually brought the trolley line to where one of West Orange's most forgotten hotels once stood.

A century ago, trolleys provided a necessary means of transportation in populated urban areas. An expanding network of tracks slowly increased trolley routes beyond just city limits. This inexpensive mode of travel soon provided accessibility to the rural countryside. Hotels often were built at the end of scenic trolley lines or rail spurs to attract patronage to increase ridership and profits. A peaceful setting away from crowded city life quickly made such destinations both desirable and, more importantly, exclusively reliant on the trolley. The City View Hotel was one such hotel in West Orange when it was built at the end of the trolley line that reached the foot of Eagle Rock in 1894, bringing accessibility to the masses.

The line began on Washington Street and found its way to Mississippi Avenue after passing through the new development of Watchung Heights built by Waston Whittlesey. From there, it made its way up Moore Terrace and up current-day Nutwold Avenue. A turn at the top ran it along the relative level grade of Mountain Avenue for a short distance. The steep grade and high elevation of Eagle Rock above Mountain Avenue made service directly to the top a difficult obstacle to overcome. The trolley line terminated below Eagle Rock at the current corner of Murray Street on Mountain Avenue. The City View Hotel located there served as a trolley terminal and featured a restaurant and outdoor café and offered lodging and vaudeville entertainment. Admission to nightly shows was free because one had to ride the trolley to get there.

A wooden staircase ascended the mountain directly across from the City View Hotel. It was known as the Hundred Steps and provided the means

A postcard shows City View Hotel bustling with activity circa 1901. *Author's collection.*

by which one actually reached the top of Eagle Rock. The steps ran on a diagonal line up the steep grade, with several short plateau levels to rest as you climbed. It's not known just how many steps there actually were, but believing there were only one hundred steps likely diminished one's perception of what could be an otherwise strenuous task. During hot summer days, the heavily shaded hillside helped make the trek bearable. Upon reaching Eagle Rock, one was rewarded with a bountiful feast for the eyes with a spectacular view still seen today. The Hundred Steps are now gone, but the former route is still partially visible to a trained eye from Mountain Avenue. The steps emerged at the top just to the right, where the concrete wall begins shortly after entering Eagle Rock. The trolley could get you close, but you had to continue on foot to get to the top.

John Cox was the proprietor of the City View Hotel, which was also once known as Cox's Hotel. In latter years, it became Underwood Brothers Café and Restaurant. It was a full two-story structure with dormers on the third floor. It featured a wraparound porch on three sides for the first two floors. Café-style tables were outside at street level, with a restaurant inside. At the far end was an outdoor waiting area for the trolley. It had a telephone and telegraph service by at least 1900. It likely only had about a dozen rooms or fewer with a shared bathroom. With the trolley line, the City View Hotel

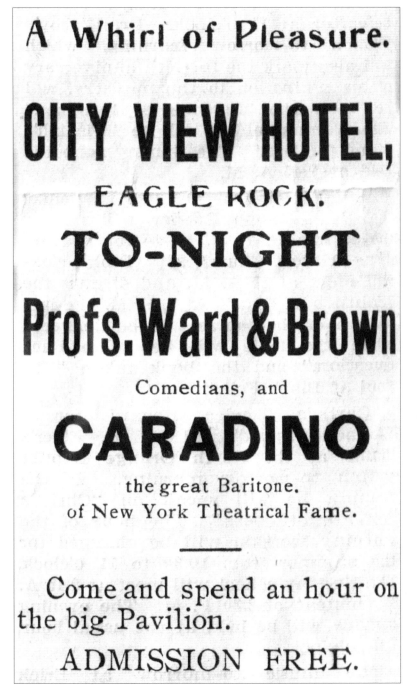

A City View Hotel ad in the *Orange Chronicle* newspaper from April 4, 1904. *Author's collection.*

became a popular destination as the perfect place to dine, socialize or just catch your breath before making the final climb to the top. Here one could spend a lazy afternoon at Eagle Rock or just relax with a dish of ice cream on the porch of the City View café. A leisurely stroll along the wooded areas on Mountain Avenue while catching a cool summer breeze was a popular activity. Overnight guests could enjoy breakfast to the sights and sounds of a peaceful Eagle Rock morning.

Operations on the newly constructed trolley line to Eagle Rock began on July 20, 1894. However, the first serious accident occurred on the line only a month after it opened. On Sunday, August 26, 1894, at 4:30 p.m., a crowded and likely overloaded trolley car left Eagle Rock with sixty passengers. From here, it came down Mountain Avenue and safely descended the steep grade of what is Nutwold Avenue today. As the car rounded the curve at the bottom of Nutwold Avenue just above present-day Amos Street, the brakes failed to hold the car, and it gained speed. At the next curve, where modern-day Nutwold Avenue meets Moore Terrace, a wheel flange broke, derailing the car and turning it on its side. There were no fatalities, but fifteen of the passengers were seriously wounded, and nearly all of them were either cut or bruised in some way. Perhaps the most serious injury was to four-year-old John Lloyd of Orange, who was pinned under the derailed car. The passengers raised the car to free the young boy, whose arm was badly mangled in the accident. It was later amputated below the elbow at Orange Memorial Hospital, where all the injured were taken. The accident left several crippled, and ensuing lawsuits totaled $172,000. After four years of litigation, the Suburban Traction Company, which operated the line, declared bankruptcy in 1898, and none of the injured ever received payment.

The line was taken over by the Orange and Passaic Valley Railway Company on July 5, 1898. Immediate measures were put into effect to make the line safer by lessening some of the severe curves and changing the track gauge. The trolley line seemed to have put the 1894 accident behind it until another serious mishap occurred. On the evening of June 5, 1903, car 51 was awaiting departure at the City View Hotel. It had reached the hotel at 9:40 p.m., and the motorman had pulled the ratchet brake taunt. He removed the brass handle, which controlled the car, and momentarily stepped into the hotel. The car's conductor had reversed the trolley pole, and car 51 was made ready for the return trip down the mountain. It remains unclear exactly how the brake was released without him returning, but the car began moving forward without a motorman.

Car 51, seen here circa 1900 in front of the City View Hotel, was destroyed in an accident on June 5, 1903. *Author's collection.*

The conductor at the rear of the car assumed the return trip was beginning and began to collect fares.

At first, the car was only running at an ordinary and expected speed, and no one noticed the absence of the motorman. But as the car rounded the first turn at the top of Nutwold Avenue, it gained dangerous speed and momentum. A concerned passenger stood up and frantically yelled at the conductor in the rear of the car, "Where is the motorman?"

This alerted the other passengers to their impending peril. The speeding car jumped the rail at the bottom of Nutwold Avenue, as many, crazed with fright, jumped off. The wooden trolley car was smashed to pieces, and only the wheels were left intact. Coincidentally, it was very near the site of the 1894 accident, and amazingly, no one was killed, although many were injured and taken to the hospital.

Following the 1903 accident, Public Service Corporation gained control of the line. The last trolley ran on April 19, 1924, after a thirty-year existence. It simply couldn't compete with the emerging technology of the automobile in the new century. It remains uncertain how long the City View Hotel stood, but it was completely gone by 1932, as indicated

Timeline

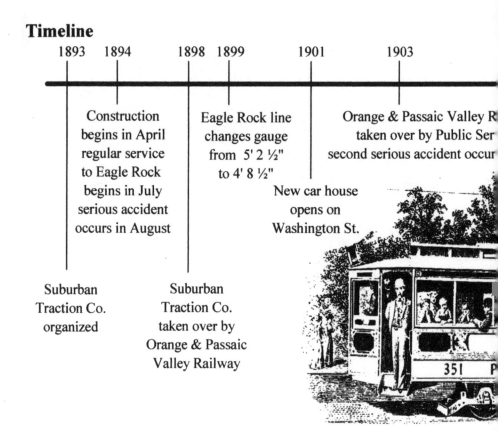

| 1893 | 1894 | 1898 | 1899 | 1901 | 1903 |

Construction begins in April regular service to Eagle Rock begins in July serious accident occurs in August

Eagle Rock line changes gauge from 5' 2 ½" to 4' 8 ½"

New car house opens on Washington St.

Orange & Passaic Valley R taken over by Public Ser second serious accident occur

Suburban Traction Co. organized

Suburban Traction Co. taken over by Orange & Passaic Valley Railway

on local maps. Without trolley service, the once-rural setting simply lost its appeal. Remnants of the Hundred Steps survived for many years after but now have all but vanished. Today, scores of motorists travel Mountain Avenue between West Orange and Montclair daily. Most are likely unaware that the homes of the quaint residential neighborhood through which they pass was an important link to a bygone era of West Orange history.

Two West Orange Train Stations

Most town residents would be surprised to learn that West Orange once had two train stations. It once was possible to catch a train on Main Street bound for New York City via a ferry at the Jersey City terminal. Both stations have

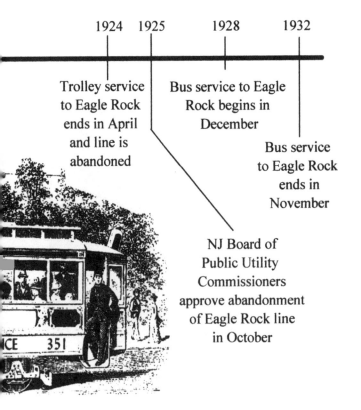

1924 1925   1928   1932

Trolley service | Bus service to Eagle
to Eagle Rock | Rock begins in
ends in April | December
and line is
abandoned

Bus service
to Eagle Rock
ends in
November

NJ Board of
Public Utility
Commissioners
approve abandonment
of Eagle Rock line
in October

Timeline of the Eagle
Rock Trolley. *Author's
collection.*

vanished, and any evidence of the railroad that once served West Orange has all but disappeared.

In 1874, a small spur line on the Greenwood Lake Division of the Erie Railroad first entered West Orange. The Watchung Branch, as it was known, began operations on July 3, 1876, to a station constructed on Park Avenue in West Orange.

It was designated as Llewellyn Station because of its proximity to the entrance to Llewellyn Park, just a short distance away on Park Avenue. This station mostly served businessmen from Llewellyn Park who needed easy access to New York City. Although easily accessible and conveniently located, the new railroad line struggled and did not become as popular as anticipated. Financial hardship loomed, and it became difficult to generate revenues. However, patronage briefly surged in 1877, when the Lackawanna line serving nearby Orange was hit with a railroad strike. During that time, the Erie provided the only means of commuting from West Orange

Llewellyn Station, seen here circa 1909, was West Orange's first train station. *Author's collection.*

or Orange. However, once the strike was settled, an overall lack of riders caused operations to cease on the West Orange Erie line on August 31, 1877, leaving the future of the railroad branch line uncertain.

Four years later, on April 11, 1881, conditions improved, new revenue prospects were found and rail operations were resumed. At that time, the line was extended from Park Avenue to Main Street and a second West Orange station was built alongside St. Mark's Church. The increasing population and growing industry of both West Orange and Orange seemed to hold new promise for the future of rail transportation in town. At this time, the Watchung Branch also became better known as the Orange Branch, even though the railroad terminated in West Orange. With the addition of the second station in 1888, the Erie Railroad first introduced express passenger service from West Orange to New York. The stationmaster at West Orange in the 1890s was William Marvel, who was credited with inventing the distinguished and recognizable Erie trademark logo in the diamond-enclosed circle.

A 1930s view of the train station on Main Street. *Author's collection.*

The Erie Railroad entered town near the West Orange/Orange border with a grade crossing across Washington Street, just a short distance past the Rosedale Cemetery. It was here in early March 1887 that a trolley running on the street from Orange known as the Crosstown Trolley wanted to cross the tracks of the Erie Railroad on Washington Street. Railroad officials denied the Crosstown Trolley permission to do so and refused to even discuss the matter. So the Crosstown Trolley took matters into its own hands and laid its track across the Erie Railroad tracks without permission in the early morning hours of March 26, 1887. Needless to say, the Erie Railroad was angered and ripped up the Crosstown Trolley tracks. The Crosstown line then decided to cross over the Erie tracks with horse-drawn streetcars. The railroad, however, was unyielding and not going to stand for this either. It decided to make life difficult for the Crosstown Trolley. The Erie then assigned a separate locomotive on a nearby siding with a full head of steam ready to go. Anytime the Crosstown Trolley approached the Washington Street crossing, the locomotive darted into action. It came to a full stop on the Erie tracks and blocked the trolley from crossing over. The issue was eventually settled in court on September 23, 1887, and the Orange Crosstown Trolley was finally permitted to cross the Erie Railroad's tracks at Washington Street in West Orange without further incidents.

The Erie's only freight yard in West Orange was located on Main Street directly opposite present-day town hall, where it served the Watchung Coal Company. A turntable used for turning the steam engines around was close by since the West Orange Station was the end of the line. Another business once located at the freight yard was the West Orange Stock Yards, owned by the Anonett brothers. It was here that live horses from out west arrived in town from the late 1880s to about 1910. They were available for sale to area residents, and experienced horsemen and cowboys were employed to handle the animals at the stockyards. West Orange High School eventually adopted the school mascot name of the cowboys and likely was inspired by the real West Orange cowboys who once worked the stockyards.

As early as 1900, the Erie railroad began losing the battle with the competing Lackawanna line in Orange. That nearby station was only a short distance away and proved to be more convenient for riders. By the 1950s, the battle was all but over. On May 20, 1955, hardly anyone noticed or cared as the last Erie passenger train pulled out of West Orange and crossed Alden Street into oblivion. With passenger service terminated, the Erie sought a new objective: to provide freight service to several industries along the right of way. This only served as a temporary reprieve because the Erie was fast approaching the end of its usefulness and may have even overstayed its welcome. Before the eventual demise, the Erie railroad served several small factories, including the industrial complex of Thomas Edison Industries. Perhaps the last surviving business once served by the railroad is today's E.L. Congdon & Sons Lumber Company on Park Avenue, where rail service first began in 1943. By the mid-1960s, only an occasional freight train could be seen in West Orange, and before the end of the decade, operations nearly ceased altogether. The two West Orange train stations had long been eyesores from years of neglect and were both torn down around 1965. Most of the rails were completely removed by the 1980s.

The Erie railroad helped play a vital role in the development of West Orange over a century ago before being slowly replaced by progress and practicality. Its existence now sits as yesterday's memory atop the scrap heap of forgotten moments in time. The majestic sounds of the iron horse chugging to a slow stop at West Orange Center have now long gone silent. We will never know the thrill of riding the rails in the bygone era of steam trains, but it's nice to imagine how our grandparents once did.

Despite the total absence of railroading in West Orange today, the last railroad car has not yet left town and still maintains a highly visible presence. In the mid-1960s, the restaurant currently known as the Essex

House on Northfield Avenue was remodeled. It originally opened there around 1937 as Rods, named after owner Rod Keller. The original interior décor of the 1960s restaurant was intended to resemble a style of the 1920s. The most impressive feature of the remodeled restaurant was an actual Pullman railroad car. The eighty-foot car was added as part of the exterior of the restaurant as an annex to the main dining room and still sits there today.

This private railroad car was originally constructed in 1909 by the Pullman Company and first went into service on the Bullfrog Goldfield Railroad in Nevada, then owned by Colonel Daniel Jackling. He was a millionaire who mined copper in Nevada and Utah. The second owner was a gin distributor named Julius Fleischman. After that, its history and reputation became clouded and tarnished when it was rumored to have been used by bootleggers during Prohibition. It was finally acquired by the Pittsburgh and West Virginia Railroad, retired from service and sat idle for many years.

In 1963, Rod Keller purchased the car, and two years later, it was transported by the Lackawanna Railroad to Madison, New Jersey, for a complete refurbishment of the finely crafted mahogany interior and crystal chandeliers. The restoration project took two months and was done by Carmine Toto at his Madison, New Jersey home with the antique railroad car sitting on jacks. Upon completion, the Pullman car was trucked in the early morning hours of September 2, 1965, to the site in West Orange. Today, the one restored railroad car with a colorful past has been part of the Northfield Avenue restaurant ever since but has seen better days and now faces an uncertain future.

Chapter 3

MURDER AND TRAGEDY

Sentenced to Death by Hanging

The image of the hangman's noose is often associated with Wild West justice, as portrayed in many Hollywood westerns. However, a man and woman living in West Orange met their fate in just that manner—at the end of a rope. Their alleged love affair led to murder, with as many subplots as a dime store romance novel.

John and Margaret Meierhoeffer were married in 1858 and moved to a twenty-seven-acre farm in 1860 in between the first and second Orange Mountains. Three years later, in 1863, this property and one-story farmhouse with a barn became part of the newly formed West Orange Township. Their property and farm fronted Northfield Avenue and was bordered by the Swamp Road, which is the current St. Cloud Avenue. Their home is now long gone but once stood near the end of present-day Sheridan Avenue on Northfield Avenue in the Essex House Restaurant parking lot. Most of Sheridan Avenue was once part of the Meierhoeffer farm.

Sometime in August 1879, a short, stocky man with a long brown beard wandered onto the Meierhoeffer farm. His name was Frank Lemmons, and he was looking for a match to light his pipe. He encountered Mrs. Meierhoeffer and engaged her in polite conversation. Apparently, Mrs. Meierhoeffer's mountain neighbors already quietly spoke about her bad reputation. She allegedly had loose habits during her husband's absence as a soldier during the Civil War. Frank Lemmons—whether knowingly or otherwise—exploited her reputation and persuaded her to hire him as a farm hand. An aging Mr. Meierhoeffer had become somewhat eccentric, limiting his ability to properly care for the farm and property. Hiring Lemmons seemed to make good sense, but this decision would ultimately prove to be a death sentence for the three of them.

Margaret Meierhoeffer and Frank Lemmons supposedly became intimately involved from the start, but after a month, Mrs. Meierhoeffer informed Lemmons that his services would be terminated. Lemmons offered to work for free in order to remain close to Mrs. Meierhoeffer, whom he found attractive. She unwisely agreed and soon learned of his intention to murder her husband. Lemmons demonstrated his plan with a loaded pistol held to Mrs. Meierhoeffer's head. Alarmed by the plot but likely unable to write in English, she dictated a note to a schoolteacher named Mr. Pearson who often bordered at the Meierhoeffer farm. She gave the note to her son, Theodore, instructing him to deliver it to a plumber named Charles Jaqui in Orange. The note contained information about Lemmons's intentions and urged Jaqui to come to the farm at once. Unable to locate the plumber, Theodore Meierhoeffer, who was unaware of the letter's urgent message, coincidentally delivered the note to Marshal Conway in Orange. Conway read the note but ignored it because he had no jurisdiction in town unless an actual crime had been committed.

Early in the afternoon of October 9, 1879, John Meierhoeffer was returning from the fields and entering the cellar of the farmhouse with a sack of potatoes. As he proceeded down the basement stairs, Lemmons followed behind and shot him point-blank in the back of the head. He dragged the body under the staircase to hide it from view. Then he instructed Mrs. Meierhoeffer to inform her son, Theodore, when he returned home that his father had gone to Newark.

Later that afternoon, Mr. Pearson returned to the Meierhoeffer farm. A frightened—and perhaps remorseful—Mrs. Meierhoeffer quietly informed Pearson what had happened. He frantically slipped away without Lemmons's knowledge to inform the authorities in Orange.

After hearing Mr. Pearson's account of the story fresh from the Meierhoeffer farm, Marshal Conway, who had previously dismissed the note warning of this tragedy, headed there with Constable Rendall and Officer O'Brien. They journeyed up the mountain by horseback and arrived just before 11:00 p.m. at the dark and isolated farmhouse. A bewildered Mrs. Meierhoeffer answered the door, and Lemmons could be seen lying in the same bed from which she had just arose. She confessed upon questioning

A TRAMP KILLS A FARMER

THE VICTIM'S WIFE A PARTY TO HIS MURDER.

The people of Orange, N. J., were shocked, on Friday morning, by the announcement that a peculiarly cold-blooded murder was committed, on the forenoon of the previous day, in an old farm-house, situated on the Northfield road, in the Orange Mountains. The victim of the tragedy was John Meierhoeffer, an elderly German farmer and dairyman, of eccentric habits. His alleged murderer is Frank Lemmons, a native of Holland, who was employed by him as a farm hand. Lemmons and Mrs. Meierhoeffer, between whom, it is alleged, criminal relations existed, have been arrested, and committed to await the action of the Coroner and the Grand Jury. Information of the murder was carried to the Orange Police-station, at 10 o'clock, Thursday evening, by J. C. Pearson, a simple-minded young man, who is teacher of District School No. 42, in West Orange. His story, in brief, was that for some time past he has boarded with Mrs. Meierhoeffer. The alleged murderer, Lemmons, was employed by her five weeks ago, and she soon became very intimate with him. Meierhoeffer, who had always acted as if he were partially insane, meanwhile went about his farm mumbling to himself, and sleeping at night in a barn. On Thursday morning, as Pearson was leaving the house to open his school, Mrs. Meierhoeffer begged him to dismiss his pupils earlier than usual. She expected trouble between Lemmons and her husband, she said, and would like to have somebody around the house. He declined to close his school earlier than usual, whereupon Mrs. Meierhoeffer requested him to write the following note at her dictation:

A newspaper account of the story from the *New York Weekly Times* on October 15, 1879. *Author's collection.*

that Lemmons had murdered her husband. At first pretending to be asleep, Lemmons then profoundly denied committing the murder, accusing a young Frenchman who lived nearby. Lemmons stated that the Frenchman was the real murderer, accusing him of coming to Mrs. Meierhoeffer to play checkers and then spending the night. A subsequent investigation revealed that story to lack any credibility.

In February 1880, Frank Lemmons and Margaret Meierhoeffer were found guilty of murder and accessory to murder and condemned to death by hanging. On January 7, 1881, the sentence was carried out at the Essex County Jail in Newark. With black hoods on and tight nooses around their necks, the trapdoor of the gallows sprang open, snapping their necks as they fell to their deaths and into a tragic and dark chapter of local history.

Murder on the Mountain

The good old days have often been thought of as simpler, trouble-free and pristine times, lacking the problems of today. Although this may hold certain truth, the dark side of humanity does not know the boundaries of time. The unsolved murder of a young West Orange girl over one hundred years ago painfully reminds us that violent crimes span the ages.

Phoebe Jane Paullin was born in Morris County in 1866, the fourth of seven children. She had three brothers and three sisters, and four other siblings who passed away before she was born. Her parents, David and Anna Paullin, moved to West Orange about 1879, and their home was located on Eagle Rock Avenue west of the quaint Pleasantdale section of today's West Orange. The house was a small two-story, weather-beaten, rickety wooden structure with a barn behind it. David Paullin earned a meager living as a shoemaker in nearby Roseland. He was a proud and distinguished-looking gentleman with white hair and whiskers who often had trouble providing for his large family. He likely supplemented his income, as most families did, by farming the fertile soil on the second mountain in the pleasant valley.

Phoebe Jane was only five foot three, but she was a physically strong girl because she was no stranger to hard labor. She was considered pretty, with dirty blonde hair, a naturally light complexion and a friendly, radiant smile. When she was only fourteen months old, she tugged on a tablecloth and accidentally pulled down an oil lamp, which struck her directly in the right eye. The injury plagued her for most of her young life, and at age fifteen, her appearance was unaffected when she received a glass eye. She had aspired to become a schoolteacher but was compelled to give it up because of a reoccurring inflammation in her good eye due to the accident.

On Saturday, November 24, 1883, at about 2:00 p.m., Phoebe left the family home in West Orange to go shopping for her mother in nearby Orange. She was handsomely dressed in a black velvet suit with a red skirt and a Basque-type jacket. On her head was a Victorian-era buckram cap trimmed with a large flowing red feather. She wore dark cotton gloves and button-up shoes suitable for walking. She bid her mother good-bye and began her journey to Orange down Eagle Rock Avenue. She was expected to return by early evening. Tragically, her family would never see her alive again.

Phoebe was last seen about 7:00 p.m., returning from Orange at the bottom of Eagle Rock Avenue near present-day Our Lady of Lourdes Church. When she hadn't returned home later that night, her parents became very concerned, but they were hopeful that perhaps she had decided to spend the night with a neighbor, Mrs. Anderson, who had previously invited her to visit. Her body was found the next morning by John Wachter and his eleven-year-old son on their way home from church while passing through Eagle Rock on their way to Monclair. The body appeared to be a discarded bundle of clothes, which caught the attention and curiosity of Wachter's young son. They were horrified by their discovery, and the Orange Police were notified because West Orange did not yet have its own police force.

Newspaper accounts report that the body was found near the entrance to the park in scrub oaks about one hundred feet off a narrow wagon road passing through Eagle Rock. It proves difficult to pinpoint the precise location since the old entrance to Eagle Rock was realigned in 1957. Pheobe traveled along an Eagle Rock Avenue that once led directly into the park. In the absence of conclusive proof, the passage of time makes stating an exact location only speculation at best. Phoebe's throat had been cut, and she bled to death. Any DNA or other evidence has long since vanished. Just days after her body was discovered, it was reported that hordes of curiosity seekers came searching for souvenirs around an unguarded crime scene, even removing flowers and plants from the site. Robbery was ruled out as a motive since her jewelry and money had not been taken. Even the items she purchased while shopping were found with her. Medical examination later revealed she had been "outraged," which was a common nineteenth-century term for raped. Several suspects were subsequently arrested and questioned in the ensuing weeks and months, but I have found no record of the actual

The entrance to Eagle Rock circa 1901, much as it looked when Phoebe Jane was found murdered in 1883. *Author's collection.*

murderer ever being brought to justice, and the case was never solved, to the best of my knowledge.

Phoebe Jane Paullin was only seventeen years old when she was buried in the family plot in West Orange's Pleasantdale Cemetery. This cemetery was originally called the Pleasant Valley Burial Ground, established about 1830. It was a privately owned cemetery founded by partners Ambrose Condit and Henry Walker. The earliest grave marker there is that of Walker's son Charles, who died in 1834 at age seven. After Ambrose Condit died in 1876 and Henry Walker in 1891, the name of the cemetery changed to its current name sometime around 1900. The descendants of the original owners in 1926 wanted the Pleasantdale Presbyterian Church located nearby to care for selected graves. The church declined since it had no jurisdiction over the graveyard. The Plesantdale Cemetery Association was then organized on July 17, 1929, and still exists today, providing perpetual care and maintenance for the grave sites.

Not far from Paullin's grave is that of another family who suffered a tragic death. The Steiner family tombstone is now badly weather-beaten and difficult to read, but their burial plot contains five family members who all died on the same day in 1918. They contacted botulism from beans they had canned themselves. Sisters Emma and Bertha were similar to Paullin in age, being only sixteen and eighteen years old.

All Phoebe Jane Paullin's hopes and dreams instantly vanished like a brisk wind, leaving her life's song unsung. She could have been anyone's daughter, sister or girlfriend with a friendly smile in today's West Orange. In another time and era, she strolled along our familiar roads of home, where she met a horrible fate. John Meierhoeffer's murder in 1879, followed by Phoebe's in 1883, likely convinced town officials to form a separate West Orange Police Department in 1884. The telling of her story is not intended to sensationalize a past tragic event but rather to fondly celebrate the life of an innocent young girl. Hopefully a greater purpose is now served by reminding us all to be forever vigilant on the road of life while honoring the memory of Phoebe Jane Paullin.

Tragedy at Home

A West Orange family lost a child in a fatal home accident almost ninety years ago. Their painfully sad story is a timeless lesson and still serves as a cruel reminder of our homes' many hidden dangers. Hopefully, heeding the warning can prevent a similar fate from befalling another family. Oftentimes, familiar surroundings create a false sense of security, but forever lurking in the shadows is the peril of a harsh reality.

James and Jennie had only been married four years when they moved into their new West Orange home at 14 North Park Drive with three young children in 1925. The evening of October 20 was probably typical for them, just as any other night when bedtime drew near. Jimmy, age four, and his sister Helen, only two and a half, likely became unruly, as most youngsters will do in preparing for bed. Perhaps a cool autumn breeze gently blowing the curtains amused the children as they finally fell fast asleep. Their parents, James and Jennie, could now find time to relax from their exhaustive daily activities with the children neatly tucked in bed. As the hour drew late, they settled in themselves with their infant daughter Elizabeth by their bedside. Before retiring for the night, they probably looked in on young Jimmy and Helen, not realizing how their peaceful innocence would soon turn to tragedy. As they fell asleep, James and Jennie had no way of knowing what would lie beyond the quite calm of that autumn night.

MURDER AND TRAGEDY

Just before dawn on October 21, 1925, Jimmy was awakened by his younger sister Helen. The two children wandered down into the kitchen while their parents and seven-month-old sister Elizabeth remained sleeping upstairs. Jimmy and Helen had gotten ahold of a box of matches from the top shelf of the kitchen closet. In 1925, matches were essential in every home

"WHAT A SHOCK, NEVER GOT OVER IT." NEEDLESS TO SAY I SPRANG UP LIKE A JACK IN THE BOX DOWN THE STAIRS FOUR AT A TIME, MET POOR HELEN WALKING UP THE CELLAR STAIRS FLAMES AS HIGH AS THE CEILING SHE WAS TRYING TO CRY BUT THE FLAMES SEARED HER LUNGS. I PICKED HER UP AND LAID HER ON THE KITCHEN FLOOR ROLLING THE FLAMES OUT WITH RHINYS OVERCOAT, THE

A handwritten account of the tragedy, written by James Fagan Sr. shortly after the accident. *Author's collection.*

for lighting the gas stove in the kitchen. The two youngsters made their way down into the basement and thrilled themselves by striking the matches. They had both been previously warned about playing with matches, but their young minds probably could not comprehend the consequences of any pending danger.

Suddenly, around 6:00 a.m., one of the matches set young Helen's nightdress on fire in the basement, and she was instantly engulfed in flames. A stunned and shocked Jimmy quickly ran upstairs to summon his sleeping father. James and Jennie were startled awake by the shouts of their frantic child crying, "Daddy, daddy, sister's on fire in the cellar!"

Confused and dazed, James Sr. arose and hurried down the stairs four at a time, where he was horrified to find his daughter ablaze at the foot of the basement stairs. She was gasping for air and couldn't breathe or cry. He grabbed an overcoat and desperately rolled the child on the floor, attempting to extinguish the flames. Grief-stricken, Jennie quickly ran to a nearby neighbor's house to phone for help since they had no telephone of their own. An ambulance soon arrived, and James was instructed to wrap his daughter Helen in a blanket. They rushed off to Orange Memorial Hospital, with James holding his dear child on his lap. Unfortunately, there was nothing anyone could have done, and she died about noon that day with her father weeping at her side. It was a sad ending for a young innocent life full of countless hopes and dreams never realized.

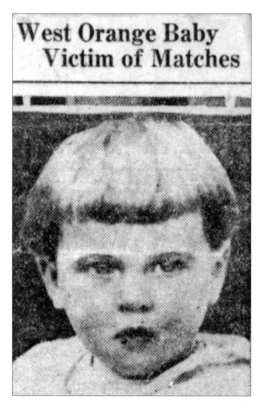

West Orange Baby Victim of Matches

A 1925 newspaper clipping showing a picture of Helen Fagan. *Author's collection.*

The funeral was held in the couple's North Park Drive home in West Orange where the accident had occurred only days before. Helen was buried in a small white coffin and lies in eternal peace at Saint John's R.C. Cemetery in Orange. A small modest grave marker was all the family could afford, and it reads, "Daughter—Helen Fagan, 1923–1925."

That little girl was the aunt I never knew, and young Jimmy grew up to become my father, who lived to see the age of eighty-two. The horror of the accident undoubtedly haunted him and my grandparents for their entire lives. But my father never shied away from an opportunity to openly talk about it and never allowed himself to drown in self-pity or guilt. He always kept the memory of his dear sister Helen close to his heart and forever on his lips. Regardless of how painful it might have been, he unselfishly knew that retelling the story could hopefully prevent the same tragedy from happening to someone else.

A little West Orange girl was sadly laid to rest many autumns ago. A ripple effect of renewed awareness traveling across the vast sea of time will perhaps honor her memory by saving the life of another child somewhere someday. I suppose the world will just never know those whose footprints through eternity will forever be unanimously woven on the tapestry of our lives.

Chapter 4

WINGS OVER WEST ORANGE

My father, James Fagan Jr., was born in 1921 and moved to a newly constructed home in West Orange in 1925 from nearby Orange, New Jersey. He would often tell me what a thrill it was for him and the other kids in their North Park Drive neighborhood to see an airplane soaring overhead. While growing up in the 1930s, they would sometimes just sit and gaze at the skies, hoping to see an airplane fly by. In those days, boasting about having seen one drew envy from those who hadn't. The youngsters of his generation were still accustomed to steam trains and horse-drawn wagons, so flying machines must have seemed truly adventurous. West Orange is a small town of just over twelve square miles, but despite being small, pilots passing above have always seemed to find it. Almost since the dawn of aviation, several incidents involving small aircraft ranging from the fatal to the bizarre have occurred here. Several famous aviators have also visited the town.

A heavy fog played a role in the first airplane crash in West Orange on April 27, 1920. It was a United States mail plane flying from Washington, D.C., to Heller Field in Newark. Amazingly, pilot Wesley J. Smith of San Francisco escaped with only minor cuts and bruises. He became disorientated with diminished visibility and crashed just east of Prospect Avenue on the farm of George Merck in Llewellyn Park. Smith was able to crawl out from under the wreckage and somehow run a safe distance before witnessing his own plane become fully engulfed in flames. He was administered first aid at the scene and badly shaken up, but he survived. The only causality was a 350-pound sack of airmail that was lost in the ensuing fire.

WINGS OVER WEST ORANGE

On the afternoon of June 10, 1942, a second plane crashed in West Orange. It went down in the Pleasantdale section of town, only about a mile away from the site of the 1920 crash. The location was a vacant field, which today is the location of the Crestmont Gardens Condominium complex on Conforti Avenue behind Pleasantdale Cemetery. The plane had left Roosevelt Field in Long Island at 1:10 p.m. and was due at Bell Laboratories in Whippany, New Jersey, at 1:50 p.m. for experimental flying. The aircraft was a Ford Trimotor biplane piloted by Richard Behrens, who was tragically killed in the crash. It exploded on impact and plunged ten feet into the ground. Many golfers on the nearby Crestmont and Essex County golf courses heard the plane and saw the fatal dive. Two of the first people on the scene were Malcolm Meyer of Irvington and Joseph Laing of West Orange, who were driving on Eagle Rock Avenue. They heard the plane sputtering overhead and witnessed the crash. They ran to the scene to attempt a rescue but were driven back by the heat of intense flames from the smoldering wreckage. The fire was eventually put out

Rescue workers gather around the plane crash in Pleasantdale on June 10, 1942. *Author's collection.*

by the West Orange Fire Department with help from the Essex Fells and Verona Rescue Squads.

On April 2, 1953, a plane equipped with pontoons intentionally made an emergency landing in the Orange Reservoir off Northfield Avenue. The plane was forced to land when a thick fog reduced visibility to zero. The crew spent the night with the aircraft, and the plane took off without incident the next morning when the fog had lifted.

On November 26, 1955, a small plane crashed at the Montclair Golf Club on Prospect Avenue near the Verona border. The pilot was Junius Wentworth Peake of Teaneck, and fortunately, he was not injured. Peake had rented the single-wing aircraft—a 1946 Aeronco Champion owned by Thomas Oran of West Orange—from the nearby Hanover Airport Flying Services Inc. Peake was returning to Hanover Airport when the aircraft developed engine trouble and forced him to safely make an emergency landing. In the 1970s, a small aircraft ran out of gas and used another West Orange golf course to make a landing, this time on the twelfth hole on the Essex County Country Club. Perhaps from the air, any open area spotted by pilots is seen as a safe landing zone for an aircraft in distress. In each incident, only minor damage was reported to both the plane and the golf course, but these events stirred equal excitement in all those who witnessed them.

On September 25, 1957, a plane was forced down at Pals Fair Ways Driving Range, once located opposite Pals Cabin restaurant. Today, the former driving range is a shopping center with a large parking lot at the northwest corner of Prospect and Eagle Rock Avenue. A New Mexico businessman crash-landed his Piper Tri-Pacer after running out of fuel. From the air, he had mistaken Caldwell Airport for his intended destination of Teterboro Airport. When he realized his error, he changed his course for Teterboro but had exhausted his fuel supply. The single-engine aircraft struck the seventy-five-yard marker on the driving range, sheared its right wing and flipped over twice. When the West Orange Police arrived on the scene, they found the occupants of the plane, Mr. and Mrs. Charles Rex Murdock, sitting next to the railing in the empty parking lot. They were both dazed and confused but walked away with only minor bruises.

On August 26, 1965, the term "green space as seen from the air" took on a coincidental meaning with a comical twist. West Orange resident David Greene was en route to Caldwell Airport in western Essex County. He was making his way home with his son after visiting his daughter Amy, who was away at summer camp in Massachusetts. Before landing at the airport, Mr. Greene asked pilot Kenneth Banga if he could kindly fly over his residence

The driving range of Pals Fair Ways, where a plane successfully landed on September 25, 1957. *Courtesy Don Horn Sr.*

on Ferris Drive in West Orange for an aerial view of his home. The house would be easy to spot from the air because it was near the first hole of the Crestmont Country Club. As the plane approached the golf course, a problem developed when the airplane's fuel pump stopped working. The aircraft suddenly began to rapidly lose altitude, and the pilot was forced to make an emergency landing. The only place to safely bring down the plane was on the golf course. The skilled pilot successfully glided the plane to a bumpy but safe landing without incident and with only relatively minimal damage to the golf course. Coincidentally, the plane came to a stop on the first hole on the Crestmont Country Club, which was almost within direct view of the Greenes' front door across the street. Mr. Greene safely exited the plane, strolled over to his house and opened the front door. His wife was sitting inside and was startled by her husband's sudden and unexpected appearance. She asked him, "How did you get here? I didn't hear the car pull up."

Mr. Greene replied, "The plane just dropped us off."

In the absence of an adequate explanation, a puzzled look came across Mrs. Greene's face. She obviously was not aware of the bizarre circumstances that got her husband safely home, nor did she understand the ironic meaning and vital importance of "Greene space as seen from the air." Mr. Greene, however, could appreciate the new lesson he had just learned: any landing you can walk away from is a good one—especially if it brings you directly to your front door in West Orange.

In September 1907, residents in nearby Montclair were startled to see the figure of a man who appeared to be falling from space above Eagle Rock. He seemed to be dangling from some sort of odd balloon that was soaring high in the sky. The airborne oddity seemed to be performing unusual acrobatic-type gyrations in midair, attracting the attention of hundreds. A curious crowd soon headed to Eagle Rock as the man suddenly began somersaulting toward earth. Many stumbled over one another in their nervous excitement to be among the first to reach the scene. Some arrived just as the man struck the ground with a loud dull thump. There was no subsequent movement from the body, and those who witnessed the landing surely felt the man had been crushed to death in the horrible plunge to earth. The stunned crowd looked on in an eerie silence. Finally, one person summoned the courage to approach the body to confirm what was surely obvious. Some in the crowd even began to sob, believing they had just seen a man plunge to his death from the sky. After turning over the body, the brave individual proclaimed that there was absolutely no sign of life. He was right because what was thought to be a man was just a well-constructed dummy. Apparently, a local youngster named Fred Hickson had succeeded in playing a carefully planned trick. Young Hickson had constructed a fairly large box kite to which he had attached the dummy. After the kite was high in the air and had attracted scores of onlookers, he pulled a release wire dropping the dummy back toward the ground. The crowd was none too pleased by Hickson's ill-conceived prank but was relieved to find out that no one had actually been killed.

On April 10, 1923, visitors to Eagle Rock would witness a real balloon landing courtesy of the U.S. Navy. Earlier in the day, a small naval balloon commanded by Lieutenant J.N. Norfleet left the Lakehurst Naval Station in southern New Jersey. Its mission was just a short observation flight, but it got carried north by a strong and unexpected head wind. As dusk approached, the men were in no danger but held out little hope for getting the airship back on course. Lieutenant Norfleet made the wise decision to safely land in the large clearing he spotted from the air, which happened to be Eagle Rock in West Orange. As the balloon approached, many hurried to the scene, thinking it was in trouble. Upon landing, Lieutenant Norfleet explained to the gathered crowd that he just needed a strong southerly wind to return safely to the

Lakehurst Naval Station. He further stated that with daylight running out, the real danger would be to be adrift in darkness. Bystanders were relieved to hear that the spectacular landing at Eagle Rock was intentional and planned. It certainly provided for an afternoon of unexpected excitement in West Orange to see such a majestic aircraft up close. No one was injured, and the crew and balloon both returned to Lakehurst by truck the following day.

Perhaps the best-known aviator of the twentieth century was Charles Lindbergh, nicknamed "Lucky Lindy." He made the first solo flight across the Atlantic Ocean on May 20 and 21 in 1927. Other pilots had crossed the Atlantic before, but Lindbergh gained international fame for being the first person to do it alone and nonstop. Only two years after his historic flight, Lindbergh visited West Orange. In August 1929, Thomas Edison invited Lindbergh, along with George Eastman, the founder of the Eastman Kodak Company, and Henry Ford, the founder of Ford Motors, to West Orange for the first-annual Edison Scholarship Contest. It was held at Edison's West Orange laboratory with forty-nine young men from states around the country competing for the Edison Scholarship Award. Edison had asked Lindbergh, along with Eastman and Ford, to be one of the judges for the

Left to right: George Eastman, Charles Lindbergh, Thomas Edison and Henry Ford at Edison's West Orange laboratories in August 1929. *Courtesy Frank Seifert III.*

contest. The ceremonies were not open to the public but caused excitement for those residents trying to get a glimpse of the world-famous Lindbergh and his wife, Anne Morrow, on Main Street.

By 1931, the idea of airplanes traveling over vast distances was still in its infancy. The record for the fastest time around the world was not even held by a fixed-wing aircraft. It belonged to the Graf Zeppelin, an airship from Germany with a record of twenty-one days set in 1929. On June 23, 1931, pilot Wiley Post and his navigator Harold Gatty set out from Roosevelt Field in Long Island to break the record in their airplane named Winnie Mae. They successfully arrived back at Roosevelt Field on July 1 after traveling 15,474 miles. They established a new record time of eight days, fifteen hours and fifty-one minutes for travel around the world. They received a reception similar to that given to Charles Lindbergh, who had flown solo over the Atlantic Ocean in 1927. Post and Gatty were welcomed at the White House by President Herbert Hoover on July 6, 1931. They rode in a ticker-tape parade the next day in New York City and attended a banquet at the Hotel Astor.

Later that month, on July 31, 1931, while on a tour of the Oranges, Wiley Post and Harold Gatty were welcomed at the old West Orange Town Hall on Northfield Avenue. They were greeted by town commissioner Frederick Erwin and Terrence Mulvey, president of the West Orange Board of Trade. Afterward, they attended a banquet held in their honor at the Essex County Country Club in West Orange.

Lindbergh, Post and Gatty were all historical pioneers in aviation history. Wiley Post and his friend, the famous American humorist Will Rogers, were tragically killed in a plane crash near Point Barrows, Alaska, on August 15, 1935. Harold Gatty passed away on August 30, 1957, and Charles Lindbergh died on August 26, 1974.

Chapter 5

TRUTH CAN BE STRANGER THAN FICTION

Beauty and the Beast

In 1933, audiences gasped in horror as film actress Fay Wray was held captive in the clenched fist of a defiant King Kong atop the Empire State Building in New York City. The movie plot proved to be a classic tale of beauty and the beast. A similar but unscripted real-life adventure once unfolded in downtown West Orange when a beauty emerged from a terrified crowd to cage the wild beast and save the day.

In 1913, across Main Street from present-day town hall bordering on White Street was the Erie Railroad freight yard. On the afternoon of May 4, 1913, three young boys on their way home entered the railroad yard. The curious trio, intending no harm, opened the door of a boxcar sitting idle on one of the sidings. The boys were startled as they unknowingly stumbled on a surprise they didn't expect. The freight yard quickly turned frightful as an angry lion jumped out of the railroad car, and the boys immediately fled in fear of their lives. Those working nearby also ran, not believing what they were seeing. The angry lion then remained in sole possession of the freight yard and could not escape because the premises were completely walled in by fences, embankments and piles of coal.

Word quickly spread, and a crowd gathered to watch the unusual sight of a lion, the so-called king of the jungle, trapped in downtown West Orange. Police officer Bernard Heslin attempted to seize control of the situation by shooting at the lion. Apparently, he was a bad shot or out of range, because the lion just yawned and seemed unfazed by the bullets dropping around him. Bordering the Erie yard at that time on Main Street was the West Orange Stock Yards. It was here that horses from out west once arrived in West Orange. The stockyards were owned by the Anonett brothers, who were experienced horsemen and cowboys. Joe Anonett was quickly called on to demonstrate his skills and lasso the ferocious lion. He brought out his lariat and skillfully slipped the rope around the beast's neck. He began to gradually reel in the lion to an uncertain fate as patrolman Heslin was taking aim to shoot it and finally end the epic saga.

At that exact moment, Lalla Selbini emerged from the crowd. She was a world-renowned vaudeville actress and an attractive woman with an eye-catching figure. She often appeared on stage in skintight outfits, pushing the limits of acceptability in Victorian high society. She was indeed beautiful but far more than just a pretty face. She was trained in both athletics and acrobatics and was considered one of the most skilled performers of her day. Her career started at age sixteen in 1894 doing bicycle stunts with a troupe of seven that included her parents. She ventured off on her own around 1904, playing theaters in both America and England. In 1911, at age thirty-two, she billed herself as the Great Lalla Selbini. Her troupe consisted of thirty people, including members of an orchestra, and elaborate expensive scenery. Her show was made up of several acts that featured her scantily clad singing and performing illusions. Her final act was entitled "The Lion's Bride" and featured a live lion on stage.

Apparently, two baggage cars of her theatrical equipment—including the lion—had arrived at the Lackawanna Orange depot on the afternoon of May 3, 1913. Her troupe had just come back from Europe and was booked at the Bijou Theatre on Main Street in Orange the following week. Upon their arrival, all her scenery was moved to the theater. However, the lion was housed in the railroad car at the West Orange Erie freight yard, away from the busier Lackawanna yard in Orange. No one counted on three mischievous boys letting it loose.

The news quickly reached Lalla Selbini in nearby Orange about the lion on the loose in West Orange. She hurried to the scene just a short distance away and arrived just in time, stepping forward before the terrified crowd. In a loud, angry voice, as if talking to her pet dog, she proclaimed, "Pete, what have they been doing to you?"

She calmly freed her trained lion Pete from the lariat that West Orange cowboy Joe Anonett had so skillfully placed around the animal. She escorted

Reconstructed newspaper ad from the *Orange Journal* in May 1913. *Author's collection.*

Pete back to the opened door of the boxcar with all the respect and dignity befitting a fellow performer. No one was more pleased than Pete, who willing jumped back up into his makeshift quarters, relieved that the ordeal was finally over. The crowd reportedly tossed their hats in the air with a resounding cheer. It was not patrolman Heslin or cowboy Joe but rather the beauty who had saved the beast. Lalla Selbini's career spanned forty years, and she once shared the stage in 1914 with the great Harry Houdini. Lalla Selbini passed away in 1943 at the age of sixty-three.

Wild West Orange Justice

Practically any evidence of a time when horses were common sights around town has now long vanished. But a tale more typically associated with frontier towns once played out on the streets of West Orange. A dispute over horses erupted on Main Street when a real cowboy imposed his own version of Wild West justice only a few generations ago.

An undated photo shows the rural nature of the West Orange Stock Yards. *Author's collection.*

West Orange likely retained its once-rural setting longer then any of the Oranges. But a new era soon dawned as hitching posts yielded to parking meters and blacksmiths were replaced by automotive repair shops. Hardly anyone seemed to notice or care as society slowly transformed from the horse and buggy to the promising modern age of the horseless carriage. West Orange was no exception and once was totally dependent on horses for motive transportation. It is perhaps hard to imagine today, but an actual western stockyard once existed across from the current West Orange Town Hall. It was run by the Amonett brothers from the 1880s until about the mid-1910s. The land is now occupied by office buildings and was once was part of the Erie Railroad freight yard.

Joe and Millar Amonett were real cowboys who received wild mustangs at the stockyard that were brought in by trains from out west. They had all the necessary skills in handling and training the horses that were offered for public sale and also provided stables where the animals could be boarded. At that time, there was a polo field located at the present-day intersection of Mount Pleasant and Gregory Avenues where Highland Place is today. It was owned and used by the Essex County Country Club when the banner sport of the club was polo, before the focus shifted to golf, as it remains today.

On the evening of October 5, 1913, Charles Munn of Llewellyn Park, West Orange, a member of the Essex County Country Club team, went to the Amonett brothers' stockyards to make an inquiry. A friend of his was a member of Point Judith Polo Team of Rhode Island and had recently played a match in West Orange against Munn's team. The Point Judith team had boarded its twenty polo ponies at the Amonett brothers' stables and received a bill for seven days' boarding. Munn was told that the bill should be for six days only and was asked to clear up the discrepancy in the interest of his friend. When Munn asked Millar Amonett why there was a boarding charge for an extra day, he was met with a harsh reply. Amonett told Munn that he was not going to reduce the charge, though Munn had only asked him to check to ensure that no mistake had been made. For whatever reason, this seemed to anger Millar Amonett, who sarcastically replied, "Perhaps you would like to have the whole charge canceled?"

Munn responded in kind and jokingly informed Millar Amonett that it would be satisfactory to do so. Millar Amonett then leaped toward Munn and slugged him in the face, knocking him to the ground. He then jumped on top of him and held him down with his knees while repeatedly punching him. Munn was a polo player and a small man and no match for the rugged cowboy Amonett, who was six foot four and 240 pounds. Fortunately for Munn, his chauffeur, Peter Chisholm, was parked nearby and overheard the conversation that had now turned ugly. Chisholm was able to pull Munn free of Amonett and perhaps even saved his life. A quick-thinking Chisholm dragged Munn back into the car and sped off to a doctor in nearby Orange. It was there that Dr. Bradshaw tended to Munn and dressed his wounds before Chisholm returned Munn back home to the safety of Llewellyn Park.

It was then that Munn notified the West Orange Police, who began a search for the cowboy Millar Amonett, who had gone missing. He was eventually located by the police and held on $1,000 bail, which he did not post. Munn, despite the beating, was not seriously harmed and subsequently decided not to press charges against Amonett. Munn further stated that he did not like or want any additional publicly over the unfortunate incident. Munn clearly was not at fault and could have rightfully brought criminal and civil charges against Amonett.

Cooler heads prevail, and unprovoked violence is never a solution to disputes. But in another time and era, a handshake between men often brought ample resolution. It's not known how, or if at all, the boarding charges for the Point Judith polo ponies were ever paid. Perhaps a grateful Millar Amonett canceled the monetary charges because Munn had canceled the criminal charges against him. It will forever remain as a forgotten chapter of real cowboys displaying some Wild West justice far from the frontier in hometown West Orange.

Fateful Decision Launches Legendary Career

West Orange mourned the passing of one of its most prominent adopted sons, Thomas Edison, at his Llewellyn Park home on Sunday, October 18, 1931. The death of the world-famous inventor attracted both national and international attention. However, an unrelated event that seemed to be of no consequence occurred the day before Edison died and would have a long-lasting impact on both the town of West Orange and the world of college football.

The most unlikely of circumstances bearing similarity to the epic clash of David and Goliath took place under a windy, dismal gray autumn sky. It was a day of youthful triumph for the boys of '31 that will forever echo their enduring legacy down through the generations. On Saturday, October 17, 1931, Dickinson College of Carlisle, Pennsylvania, played Penn State in football on its home field. Dickinson College was a smaller school in both enrollment and resources. The two schools had met annually from 1896 through 1907. Penn State held the upper hand with a 7-4-1 series record against Dickinson and had shut it out four straight years, including a 52–0 rout on November 2, 1907. The 1931 game would be the last meeting ever between the two Pennsylvania schools. The ensuing decades have not faded the memory of Dickinson's unlikely 10–6 victory over the Nittany Lions that brisk October afternoon, and it is still affectionately recalled as the team's finest hour.

The captain of the 1931 team was Ed Johnson, who had the honor of wearing a sweater with a big D on it representing Dickinson. This distinguished him from his teammates, who only wore the school colors on their sweaters. The concept of numbers on both sides of football sweaters would eventually evolve into jerseys as we know today, but player numbers were not yet used at this time. Johnson had shocked the crowd by nearly scoring on the opening kickoff. He was stopped at midfield by the last Penn State defender between him and the end zone. Following the hard-fought contest and unexpected victory, Johnson phoned his girlfriend, Laura, back at the college to tell her Dickinson had beat Penn State. Laura would later become Johnson's wife and mother of their four children.

Following graduation, Johnson coached football at Elmer L. Meyers High School in Wilkes-Barre, Pennsylvania, before serving in the U.S. Navy. While he was away serving his country, tragedy struck the Johnson family. Their only son at the time, Richard, was burned in an accident at home and passed away. Ed and Laura sought to put the incident behind them by seeking a fresh start in new surroundings. It remains unclear exactly why, but they decided to come to West Orange. They made their home on Lawrence Avenue, and Ed was hired by the West Orange School system. He eventually became the principal at Edison Junior High School and was the principal when I attended Edison Jr. High School in 1971. I never knew that a decision he once made would arguably have a profound impact on the world of college sports.

Ed Johnson had remained friendly with many acquaintances in the world of college football. He was best remembered as the team captain who beat Penn State in 1931 and was well liked and respected. His experience and knowledge spawned opportunity, and in 1950, he was offered a job as assistant football coach at Penn State, his former opponent. Since he liked his home in West Orange and the steady paycheck he was making, he turned it down. Penn State head football coach Rip Engel was forced to find someone else for the job that he first offered to Johnson. Engel found a young and energetic coach by the name of Joe Paterno. Had Ed Johnson accepted the position at Penn State, the entire trajectory of college football history and of Paterno as the iconic coach might have been different.

Ed Johnson passed away on June 24, 2006, as a retired educator at the age of ninety-seven. Soon after, Ann Johnson Jobbins, one of his three daughters, decided with her family to donate Ed Johnson's cherished team captain sweater to the college. On October 14, 2006, Ann and a dozen family members, including several of Ed's grandchildren, gathered at Dickinson's Sports Hall of Fame for a ceremony. She donated his 1931 football sweater worn during the Penn State game to the same Hall of Fame to which Ed Johnson had been inducted in 1972. The sweater now joins the game football on permanent display at Dickinson College in Carlisle as a testimony to a game remembered through the ages.

History so often lies in the fringes of our everyday life, just waiting to be discovered. I only regret that I missed the opportunity to ask my former principal Ed Johnson about his experience. But I fondly remember him as a soft-spoken man with a captivating smile and an unassuming role in college history that I just never knew.

Path to Stardom Passes through West Orange

Wladziu "Walter" Valentino Liberace left his West Allis suburban Milwaukee home in Wisconsin hoping to pursue a promising career as an entertainer. He had no way of knowing what heights he would one day achieve. The road to fame and fortune began for him in West Orange, and the world would come to know him only as Liberace.

In 1941, Marty Horn Sr., the owner of the Pals Cabin restaurant, was looking to hire a pianist for the old Spinet player in the restaurant. Jay Mills, a friend of Horn, was the entertainment agent for Pals at the time. Mills advised Horn that there was a sensational young kid from Milwaukee who was a budding pianist. His name was Walter Liberace, and he was looking to jump-start his career somewhere in the spotlight of New York on the East Coast. Horn took Mills's advice and proceeded to book Walter for a one-year engagement beginning in January 1941. Living arrangements were made for Walter to reside at the Mills home in nearby Glen Ridge at that time.

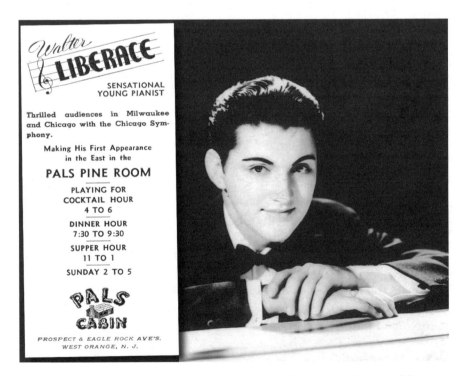

An original ad from Pals Cabin restaurant alongside a publicity photo of a young Liberace at the restaurant. *Author's collection. Photo courtesy Don Horn Sr.*

In anticipation of Walter's arrival, Horn decided to replace the Spinet piano with one more fitting for such a talented and gifted player. Horn contacted Ed Leach, another friend who owned a warehouse in Verona, New Jersey. Leach sold Horn a 1924 concert grand Steinway piano for $600. It was a steep price in those days but an investment that eventually would pay off for Horn. While Walter Liberace played at Pals Cabin, his weekly salary was $40, $30 of which he sent home to his mother, and he took on babysitting jobs locally to earn extra money.

I met with Don Horn Sr. at Pals Cabin on several occasions before it closed in 2013. His father, the late Marty Horn Sr., was the co-founder of the landmark West Orange restaurant in 1932 with his then partner Roy Sale. Both Horn and Sale were childhood pals, and their relationship spawned the restaurant's name.

The Horn family ran Pals Cabin for more than eighty years until it closed and was torn down. Don's brother Marty Horn Jr. sadly passed away, and Don, in his early eighties, still has vivid memories of when Walter Liberace played there at age twenty-two. Don still talks about it as if it were only yesterday.

He fondly recalls Walter as a great guy and nice person. He explained how he was always very polite and neat and always wore a black tuxedo when he played. After all, he was only a kid starting out and living away from home for the first time. At that time, he played only classical music, which faded into the background and created a pleasant ambiance while patrons dined at the restaurant. Don and his brother Marty also received private weekly piano lessons directly from Liberace in exchange for a weekly Thursday night dinner Mrs. Horn would serve at their West Orange home. Don explained how even then, Liberace exhibited signs of greatness before he was a household name. Don says, "He was more than a really good piano player because he also knew how to be great showman."

After Liberace's yearlong commitment at Pals, he moved on to become a staff pianist for a New York City radio station. By the late 1940s, he was performing at nightclubs in major cities around the country. He had mostly abandoned the classical format and evolved into more of a showman, with fancier outfits and his trademark candelabra. By the 1950s, he was on his way to stardom, earning more than $50,000 a year playing in Las Vegas, Nevada.

Years later, Liberace once returned to the area when he played the Meadowbrook in Cedar Grove, New Jersey. Mrs. Horn sat in the front row and greeted him when he walked on stage, saying, "Hello Walter."

The original Steinway piano used by Walter Liberace, as seen in Pals Cabin in 2012. *Author's collection.*

By that time, the performer had dropped his first name of Walter and was only known as Liberace. He acknowledged her with a smile and jokingly responded with the typical quick wit that was the Liberace style, "Someone here knows my maiden name."

In later years, Liberace often referenced his start at a small New Jersey restaurant but rarely, if ever, mentioned Pals Cabin by name.

The famous and historic Steinway piano once used by Walter Liberace proudly sat in plain view in the Tap Room at Pals Cabin until the recent closing. It had been rebuilt several times and had not been in the exact same location in the restaurant when used by Liberace. Back in Liberace's day, it was located in the Winchester Room in a small alcove that once existed in the wall.

Liberace's final stage performance was at Radio City Music Hall in New York on November 2, 1986. He passed away on February 4, 1987, at his winter home in Palm Springs, California. He emerged as a world-famous entertainer who launched his career on the East Coast with fondly remembered and humble beginnings at West Orange's Pals Cabin.

Romantic Interest Discovered in West Orange Impacts History

Local remnants of presidential history are often obscured by the spotlight of attention cast on a national level. But West Orange played a forgotten role as the crossroads of the families of two former presidents. It was here that the Hyde Park Roosevelt family of Franklin Delano Roosevelt crossed paths with the Oyster Bay Roosevelt family of Theodore Roosevelt.

Douglas Robinson Sr. and his wife, Fanny Monroe Robinson, came to West Orange about 1872, becoming neighbors to General George McClellan along the ridge adjacent to Prospect Avenue. In 1882, their son Douglas Robinson Jr. married Corinne Roosevelt, the sister of Theodore Roosevelt. Douglas and Corinne soon became frequent visitors to the seventy-two-acre estate in West Orange known as Overlook, and in 1886, their second child was born there. Douglas Robinson Jr. inherited the West Orange property in 1893 when his father passed away. At first, it was only used as a summer retreat as the family divided their time between West Orange, New York City and another home in upstate New York. But by 1894, Corinne Roosevelt Robinson so loved the country setting of Overlook that she persuaded Douglas to make the West Orange estate their principal residence. The Robinsons and their four children then moved to West Orange and lived here year round from 1894 to 1911.

Corinne soon became known as the "Queen of the Orange Mountain" as she hosted lavish parties and frequent Roosevelt family gatherings. All members of the Roosevelt family came to West Orange at one time or another. Theodore Roosevelt visited West Orange several times and stayed with his sister Corinne. As vice president, he attended a reception at the West Orange High School, then located on Gaston Street, on July 1, 1901.

Perhaps one of the most fateful events to impact the future of American history occurred at the West Orange home of Douglas and Corinne Robinson. They hosted a Roosevelt family Christmas party in 1898, where a young man asked his younger cousin Anna to dance. It likely was not the first time the two had met, but it would be their most memorable. Since they were distant cousins, they had likely been acquainted with each other at previous family gatherings. It was here in West Orange that Franklin Delano Roosevelt, age sixteen, had first taken a romantic interest in his younger distant cousin Anna Eleanor Roosevelt, who was only fourteen. From this encounter and first dance together in West Orange, a romance blossomed. It is documented in a 1971

Eleanor and Franklin Roosevelt much as they looked in 1898 when they first discovered their romantic interest for each other. *Courtesy Franklin D. Roosevelt Library.*

book written by Joseph Lash, who could be considered the foremost expert on Eleanor and Franklin Roosevelt. Lash even specifically mentions West Orange by name. The cousins' interest only increased as they ran into each other at various social events in New York City.

In conducting some additional research, I found that the surviving papers of Corinne Roosevelt Robinson are currently housed in the archives of the Harvard College Library in Cambridge, Massachusetts. I decided to take a trip there in September 2013 to see what else I could find. I spent two days at the Houghton Library on the Harvard campus looking through boxes of her letters, diaries and other papers searching for additional West Orange references. I was pleased to find many and gained a deeper insight into her days in West Orange. Perhaps the most telling was a journal signed and dated by guests to Overlook in West Orange. There I found Eleanor's signature in the journal, confirming her attendance at the 1898 Christmas party. Franklin neglected to sign the guest book, but his attendance at the 1898 party is documented in Lash's book. I did find that Eleanor and Franklin Roosevelt were both present several other times at Overlook and had both signed the guest book on other occasions. It all gives further evidence of their continuing romance that began in West Orange in 1898.

Their relationship grew increasingly more serious, and Franklin proposed to Eleanor on November 22, 1903. Franklin's mother, Sara Roosevelt, was concerned that they were too young to get married and asked them to keep the engagement secret for a year. Franklin Delano Roosevelt gave Eleanor Roosevelt an engagement ring on her twentieth birthday on October 11, 1904. They finally announced their engagement at family gatherings beginning in early December 1904. Eleanor Roosevelt was walked down the aisle and given away to Franklin Delano Roosevelt, her fifth cousin once removed, by her Uncle "Teddy," President Theodore Roosevelt, when they married on March 17, 1905, at the White House.

Franklin and Eleanor discovered their romantic interest in West Orange while visiting the home of Eleanor's Aunt Corinne. One can only imagine how both their pivotal roles in American history on a national stage might have been altered if not for that first fateful meeting, which is deeply interwoven into our own local history.

Chapter 6

THOMAS EDISON

Iconic Image of West Orange

W hen Thomas Edison first arrived in West Orange, he was already wealthy and famous, being widely known as the "Wizard of Menlo Park." That was where he invented the phonograph in 1877 and perfected the electric light bulb in 1879. Following the death of his first wife, Edison married twenty-one-year-old Mina Miller, the daughter of a wealthy midwestern manufacturer, on February 24, 1886. He offered his new bride a choice between a town house in New York City or a quiet home in the suburbs. Mina knew how deeply committed her husband was to his work. She decided it would be better for him to live closer to a new laboratory complex proposed for West Orange. Besides, she likely preferred the less hectic lifestyle that a quiet estate could offer in West Orange. Edison purchased the Glenmont home fully furnished in Llewellyn Park as a wedding gift for his new wife. Thomas Edison secured 1,093 U.S. patents in his life and endures as the iconic image of West Orange. He lived here until his death in 1931. His former West Orange laboratories and Llewellyn Park home are now part of the Thomas Edison National Historical Park.

Edison's Llewellyn Park home, Glenmont, shines in the light of some often overlooked history. The home is set on well-manicured grounds, glowing with a stunning presence. The twenty-nine-room red brick and wood mansion was designed by architect Henry Hudson Holly in the American Queen Anne style. It was built in 1880 with recognizable features such as the asymmetrical façade, steeply pitched gables, a rooftop balcony and the wraparound porch, with a unified color throughout the exterior elements.

Henry C. Pedder built the mansion six years before Edison purchased it. Pedder's infamous story has long been overshadowed by Thomas Edison and is an interesting and often forgotten footnote to history. Pedder was working for Arnold Constable & Company as an accountant, or confidential clerk, as it was then known. Arnold Constable & Company was the first department store and the oldest operating in the United States from 1825 to 1975. Pedder secretly embezzled funds estimated at $300,000 from the firm. With this money, he built and furnished Glenmont. Pedder apparently spared no expense on interior elements such as stained-glass windows, chandeliers, eloquent wainscoting and elaborate wood workings, all done with the finest craftsmanship of the day. Pedder also had a library built off the entrance foyer and filled it with over one thousand books. The impressive embellishments to the home were all for just lavish decoration. When President Garfield was assassinated in 1881, Pedder wrote a book at Glenmont entitled *President Garfield's Place in History*. Although the book was intended to honor Garfield, it was poorly written and not well received.

Pedder recklessly spent money in building the house without reservation about concealing it and was openly living far above his means. Because of this, Pedder eventually drew suspicion, and his misdeeds were uncovered in 1884. He had just returned to West Orange from a European trip when he was confronted with the evidence. Remarkably, his employer, the Arnold Constable & Company, was willing for Pedder to escape prosecution. The company forced Pedder to sign the Glenmont home and grounds over to it for the sum of one dollar. Pedder and his wife, Louisa, had no children, but his sister-in-law, a widow, lived at Glenmont with her children. Pedder and his extended family then left West Orange in disgrace and reportedly moved to Barbados, never to be heard from again.

In 1885, the Arnold Constable & Company sold Glenmont fully furnished to Edison for the sum of $235,000, roughly half its value. The three children from Edison's first marriage all came to live at Glenmont. He and Mina subsequently had three more children—Madeleine, Charles and Theodore—all born in West Orange. A few of Edison's many distinguished guests at his Llewellyn Park home included Orville Wright, Helen Keller, Henry Ford, Harvey Firestone and Charles Lindbergh. Edison died at Glenmont on October 18, 1931. Mina remarried in 1935 to her childhood friend Edward Everett Hughes, who joined her at Glenmont. Everett died in 1940, and it was Mina's last wish before she passed away in 1947 that Glenmont would one day would be a museum honoring her famous first husband.

Glenmont, Llewellyn Park, West Orange, circa 1905. **Courtesy** *Thomas Edison National Historical Park.*

Although most town residents may be familiar with the site of Edison's former laboratory, there is an oddly shaped small black building near the entrance. It likely does not call much attention to itself because it is far from glamorous and often misunderstood. But it stands as a tribute to the Edison genius and the film industry of today that he helped create. His former Main Street complex in West Orange gave birth to the world's first motion picture studio. The small tarpaper-covered building is the size of a bungalow and was first built in 1893. It was specially designed on a track so it could be rotated with the roof open to keep it aligned with the sun. The film speed was so slow that only natural sunlight would work. The inside walls of the studio were painted black, helping to eliminate reflections and created needed contrast between actors and the background. The studio was dubbed the Black Maria (pronounced Ma-*rye*-a) by those who worked there. Since it was a small and uncomfortable place to work, it reminded his employees of Black Marias, which were the common name for the cramped police vans also known as paddy wagons. Edison's own name for the building was the "doghouse."

By the late 1880s, the concept of moving images as entertainment was not a new one and didn't belong solely to Edison. The films produced at the Black Maria were not films as we know them today but were specifically for use in one of Edison's inventions, the Kinetoscope. This device sat on the floor and required the user to insert a coin and look into it while standing. It was commonly referred to as a peep show. The first Kinetoscope parlor opened in New York City on April 14, 1894. For a total of twenty-five cents, a customer could view the films in all five machines, which were neatly placed in a row. Kinetoscope parlors soon increased in popularity and opened around the country. Constant production of a flow of new films was needed at the West Orange studio to keep the new invention popular. Many vaudeville performers, dancers and magicians became the first entertainers to be filmed at the Black Maria. Subjects also included acts from Buffalo Bill's Wild West Show, including Annie Oakley, who visited West Orange with a troupe of Native American dancers. Other films were intended to appeal to mostly male audiences, with boxing and cockfights, and at times, they even featured scantily clad women. During 1894, over seventy-five of these motion pictures were made in West Orange at the Black Maria studio.

By 1895, sales of Kinetoscopes began to slow down, mostly due to competing technology that developed and used projected motion pictures as we know today. To compensate for the declining popularity of the Kinetoscope, in April 1895, Edison developed the Kinetophone. It was Edison's attempt to combine a moving picture with sound from a phonograph and make talking pictures a reality. However, the device could not achieve exact synchronization and ultimately failed to find a market. Edison was slow to realize that films projected for large audiences could generate more profits because fewer machines were needed. By January 1901, Edison had focused his efforts toward work on conventional motion picture projection. He opened a new studio in the Bronx, bringing a final end to the Black Maria–studio era in West Orange.

The original Black Maria studio was constructed in 1893 for a total cost of $637.67 and was torn down sometime around 1903. In May 1940, a temporary reproduction was built near the site to coincide with the release of the film *Edison the Man*, starring Spencer Tracy and Rita Johnson. The reproduction was short-lived and was dismantled following the film's debut. In 1954, the current Black Maria now standing at the Thomas Edison National Historical Park was built very near the original location at a cost of $25,000. During the years when it was used by Edison, the original Black Maria studio had undergone various changes in appearance, having been both lengthened and shortened. The current reproduction is a representative and fully functional example of how it once looked and worked.

The Kinetoscope parlors featuring Edison's remarkable new invention often attracted crowds and long lines to see films that only had an average

Thomas Edison and wife Mina pose with the class of 1926 at West Orange High School.
Author's collection.

length of forty seconds. This early commercial success seemed to pass into history almost as quickly as it had appeared, but West Orange will forever hold historic and significant relevance as the birthplace of today's worldwide film industry.

Edison's landmark laboratory grew to become a sprawling research and development center and home to many experiments and inventions. But perhaps lesser known and equally important are some other sites in West Orange where Thomas Edison once conducted secret experiments during World War I involving submarine warfare.

The Naval Consulting Board was established in 1915 by then Secretary of the Navy Josephus Daniels. The board was organized during World War I, nearly two years before the United States entered the war raging in Europe. Its purpose was to use the established machinery and facilities of business leaders of American industry. Daniels was concerned that the United States was unprepared for the new anticipated conditions of naval warfare should the United States be drawn into the growing conflict. It was hoped that ingenuity and know-how could create new technology specifically for combating the increasing threat of submarine warfare. Thomas Edison became chairman of the Naval Consulting Board, which had twenty-four members, including fellow New Jersey inventor Hudson Maxim.

In March 1916, the invention of a sixteen-year-old West Orange High School student caught Edison's attention. Orlando Angelillo, born in Italy in 1900, had presented to Edison the means by which it was possible for a ship at sea to detect submarines underwater. The device was tested at Cable Lake in West Orange, which is near the current clubhouse of the Rock Spring Country Club. Edison believed the idea had merit and could be useful and advised Angelillo that the idea should be presented before the entire Naval Consulting Board. The exact nature of the device was not disclosed at the time, and it still remains unclear precisely how it was developed, what it was or if it was ever implemented. However, nearly one year later, in February 1917, Edison was reported to have a sixteen-foot working model of a submarine. It was said to have been housed near the Edison Plant in a corrugated iron building on Columbia Street. The building had the windows barred and coated to maintain security and secrecy. It is not known if this project was at all related to the youngster Orlando Angelillo's invention for detecting submarines.

However, also in February 1917, Thomas Edison was granted permission by the then Essex County Park Commission to conduct experiments in the Eagle Rock Reservation. The second floor of the casino, which opened at Eagle Rock around 1910, became the Eagle Rock laboratory of Edison. The casino, which was nearly torn down in the 1980s due to vandalism and neglect, eventually became today's Highlawn Pavilion Restaurant in 1985. But in 1917, guards patrolled the grounds at Eagle Rock, where Edison and his men usually worked late into the night. Special machinery was installed that required heavy cables using considerable electrical power. The *New York Times* reported that Edison's Eagle Rock laboratory was equipped nearly as well as his Main Street laboratory. The men working there were nicknamed the "insomnia squad" because they sometimes did not leave the building for days at a time. The project was classified as top secret but was believed to be a device by which the operator could shine a light from aboard ship and view a great distance at sea, but it was invisible and undetectable from the point from which it was aimed. Other experiments were also being conducted outside on the open fields at Eagle Rock during this time. It remains unclear exactly what devices or apparatuses were developed as a result of this work. But these experiments could have served as a body of work that aided in

Edison detonates a test explosive under the pedestrian bridge in the abandoned rock cut of the cable road on June 13, 1917. *Courtesy Wade Knowles.*

the research and development of weapon systems eventually adopted by the U.S. Navy.

Another West Orange location once used by Thomas Edison was the deep rock cut of the once-majestic Cable Road. Here, cable cars once passed from the Orange Valley to the top of the mountain near the current Rock Spring Country Club.

By July 1917, the rock cut was abandoned, and Edison used the secluded site in West Orange to conducted experiments below the ornamental iron bridge. Here he performed test explosions looking to produce shells for the navy that could be fired from merchant ships as a defensive measure. This projectile could be used against submarines to hide the ship and eliminate the threat of being fired on. The results of these West Orange test explosions were sent to Josephus Daniels, secretary of the navy, in a report that Edison labeled Report # 41.

Thomas Edison is almost always associated solely with his Main Street laboratories because of their highly visible presence. However, during

World War I, several West Orange locations played an immeasurable and often forgotten role in keeping the world safe for democracy. Also, while the winds of World War II were raging in Europe, West Orange residents briefly welcomed a distraction from the quickly developing world events. Hollywood came to town for the world premiere of a movie featuring West Orange's Thomas Edison.

In 1940, MGM Pictures produced two movies depicting the life of inventor Thomas Alva Edison. The first movie, *Young Tom Edison*, staring Mickey Rooney, chronicled Edison's boyhood to age twenty-two. It made its world premiere in the childhood hometown of Edison in Port Huron, Michigan, on February 10, 1940. Three months later, the sequel to the movie, titled *Edison the Man* and starring Spencer Tracy and Rita Johnson, made its world premiere. Although MGM decided to do so near West Orange where Edison once lived, the movie missed the mark on key points.

The movie premiered on May 16, 1940, at the Hollywood Theater once located on Central Avenue in East Orange. At the time, West Orange had two movie theaters of its own, and the Llewellyn Theater on Main Street was within sight of Edison's former laboratories. The movie only told the story of Edison up to the time that his first wife, Mary Stilwell, died in 1884. The movie ended without including Edison's second marriage to Mina Miller in 1886 and included no mention of him moving to West Orange in 1887. The script was also highly fictionalized; all of the characters outside Edison's immediate family were made up.

Despite these factual inaccuracies, the movie was nominated for an Academy Award for best writing, but it did not win. At the night of the premiere at the Hollywood Theater, some five thousand people braved a windswept rainstorm to attend the event. All wanted to catch a glimpse of legendary actor Spencer Tracy and his co-star Rita Johnson on the red carpet as they made a personal appearance at the opening.

Two of the attendees at the movie's premiere that night were my late aunts Betty (née Dyer) and her sister Peggy (née D'Heron) Fagan. Because of the heavy rain, my grandfather James Fagan Sr. decided to drive them to the theater. He pulled his car right up to the front entrance and was briefly blocking the entrance to the red carpet. This might not have been a problem, but as fate would dictate (and unknown to my grandfather), Spencer Tracey and Rita Johnson were in the car directly behind him. Assisting with crowd control at the scene that night was police officer William Rooney of West Orange. Rooney quickly approached my grandfather's car, lightly tapping it with his nightstick and instructing him to move. My grandfather, not realizing that Spencer Tracy

The scene outside the Hollywood Theater on the night of the premiere, possibly showing police officer William Rooney in the foreground. *Courtesy Thomas Edison National Historical Park.*

and Rita Johnson were behind him, refused to budge, ignoring Rooney's request. My grandfather yelled to Rooney that he wasn't moving until both his daughters, Betty and Peggy, were safely out of the car. However, once both girls exited the car, the officer and my grandfather continued to quarrel.

Tempers flared, and both my grandfather and Rooney allowed the mild misunderstanding to escalate instead of quietly going their separate ways. Somehow, amid the excitement and turmoil, my grandfather and Rooney agreed to meet at some future date in the Eagle Rock Reservation for a boxing match to settle the issue between them. My grandfather then moved the car, and Spencer Tracy and Rita Johnson entered the theater on the red carpet. The adoring fans were oblivious to the unexpected delay caused by Grandpa Fagan's words with Rooney.

Cooler heads prevailed, and they never did meet at Eagle Rock for their boxing match. Both men simply got caught up in the excitement and frustration of a moment filled with confusion during a driving rainstorm. William Rooney lived to fight a far more important battle and was tragically killed in the South Pacific in 1944 during World War II. Rooney Circle at the Essex Green Shopping Center is now named in his honor. My grandfather

The large picture of Thomas Edison as it appeared on the steps of West Orange Town Hall. *Courtesy Dorothy Robertson.*

James Fagan Sr. also served in the war with the U.S. Navy and passed away in 1965. No street bears his name, although had he boxed Rooney, there might be a James Fagan Memorial Drive at Eagle Rock today, commentating his early demise from the fight with Rooney.

The showing of the movie actually concluded a three-day affair celebrating the life of Edison. It began with the unveiling of what was billed as the world's largest photo. A two-story picture of Edison hung over the front steps of West Orange's Town Hall. Some twelve thousand people converged on town hall to see the film's co-star, Rita Johnson, flick a switch with Edison's widow, Mina, that turned on seventy thousand watts of light illuminating a very large image of Thomas Edison on the steps of West Orange Town Hall for the entire world to see.

Prior to the unveiling, Spencer Tracy had stopped in at West Orange Town Hall to chat with Francis Byrne, who was the police commissioner in town at the time. At that private meeting was Byrne's young son Brendan and Charles Edison. He was the son of Thomas Edison and served as the forty-second governor of New Jersey from 1941 to 1944. Brendan Byrne went on to become another gubernatorial resident from West Orange, joining Edison, George McClellan and Richard Codey. Byrne served two terms as New Jersey's forty-seventh governor, from 1974 to 1982. I asked Brendan Byrne in a recent interview about that fateful meeting with Edison

Charles Edison is seen casting a vote for himself for New Jersey governor at the Gaston Street School in West Orange on May 21, 1940. *Author's collection.*

at West Orange Town Hall in 1940. A smile grew across Governor Byrne's face when I asked him if he ever thought as a young boy that he would one day have Edison's job. He said it was exciting to meet Spencer Tracy and vividly recalled shaking Edison's hand but only regrets his father Francis Byrne never saw him elected governor, having passed away shortly before he was elected.

Charles Edison was the only former New Jersey governor actually born in West Orange at Glenmont, his parents' Llewellyn Park home, on August 3, 1890. Prior to his election as governor, he served as both assistant secretary and acting secretary of the navy, having been first appointed by President Franklin Roosevelt on January 18, 1937. He became associated in business with his aging father in 1927 as president of Thomas A. Edison Incorporated and ran the company following his father's death in 1931 until the company was sold in 1959. Charles Edison passed away ten years later on July 31, 1969, in New York City, where he lived at the time, and is buried in the Rosedale Cemetery in Orange.

Thomas Edison passed away on October 18, 1931, at his West Orange home in Llewellyn Park, where he had been near death for almost ten days. At times, Mr. Edison displayed amazing vitality but would fade into a deep coma-like sleep. He seemed to be on the cusp of dying many times before it actually happened. Only the day before, household servants and old employees were taken to him in the afternoon for a last good-bye. When it became apparent that Edison was finally fading away, Dr. Hubert Howe quickly summoned the family to his bedside. Present in the room were Mrs. Edison and their three children, Charles, Theodore and Madeleine. Also present were the three children from Edison's first marriage, Thomas

The hometown newspaper of Thomas Edison announces the news of his death. *Author's collection.*

Jr., William and Marion, with two assisting nurses. Several other people, including Mrs. Edison's brother and sister and their spouses, along with other friends, waited outside the room to receive final word that he had passed. Dr. Hubert recorded the exact time of death as 3:24 a.m., and news of his passing was soon released to the world.

During this trying time, Charles Edison had been in constant communication with the White House in Washington, D.C., from West Orange. When his father had passed away, he phoned the White House to deliver the message to the president. The message was wired to President Hoover, who was at sea aboard the USS *Arkansas* when he received word of the inventor's passing in West Orange. It's interesting to note the phone number at Glenmont at the time of the passing of Edison. Only a year before, with the number of household phones growing throughout the Oranges, several new phone exchanges were created. At that time before direct dialing, to place a call, you spoke to an operator and gave the number to which you wanted to be connected. Sometime in 1930, Glenmont received the phone exchange of Nassau. Edison apparently had the privilege of being the first home served by the new exchange and was given the phone number of Nassau 1.

Then mayor of West Orange Simeon H. Rollinson ordered all flags in town to be flown at half staff and issued the following public statement: "In the death of Thomas Edison the Town of West Orange has lost its most prominent and useful citizen. His death has not only caused a loss to the town but to the nation and the whole civilized world. I wish, as Mayor of West Orange, on behalf of its officials and citizens, to express to the family of Thomas A. Edison our deepest and most sincere sympathy."

It was announced on the Monday following his death that Thomas Edison would lie in state at his Main Street laboratory. An estimated crowd of ten thousand people had gathered during the day to pay their respects. On Tuesday, the public viewing had been intended to remain open only until 6:00 p.m., but there were so many people gathered in line and wrapped around Lakeside Avenue that Mrs. Edison decided to leave it open all night until early the next day. It was estimated that more than fifty thousand people viewed Edison's coffin in his West Orange laboratory. A private viewing was subsequently held at Glenmont and attended by about four hundred people, mostly family and friends. Thomas Edison was laid to rest at the Rosedale Cemetery in Orange. The grave of the world-renowned inventor was eventually moved, and today both Thomas and Mina Edison lie together in eternal rest in the shadow of their former home on the Glenmont grounds in West Orange's Llewellyn Park.

Edison's former laboratory and home firmly preserve his legacy, and several local stories about him have been passed down through ensuing generations of West Orange residents, and here are but a few. Sonny Ciamillo, (see Chapter 9) now ninety-one years old and retired, grew up in

West Orange and worked for the town for more than fifty-three years. Sonny shared his personal experience with me about when, as a young boy, he saw Edison walking along Main Street. Sonny still vividly recalls how on several occasions, Edison stopped to buy him and his friends ice cream. Longtime West Orange teacher and track coach Joe Suriano, for whom Suriano Stadium at West Orange High School is named, shared with me the story about his father-in-law, Nelson Melillo. Nelson was only eight years old and was walking along Lakeside Avenue when a gray-haired elderly gentleman who turned out to be Thomas Edison patted him on the head and gave him a coin.

My own father, James Fagan Jr., grew up in West Orange but never met Edison. However, he and his lifelong friend Ken Tinquist lived near Llewellyn Park and often recounted for me how Mrs. Edison would give them both a ride in her electric car, now on display at the Glenmont museum. Even the Fagan name will forever remain enumerated along with Thomas Edison. A church history book from St. John's in Orange lists alphabetically my great-grandfather Richard Fagan immediately following Thomas Edison's name for having made a fifty-dollar donation to the church's Golden Jubilee fund in 1919.

The name of Edison is forever firmly planted in the conscience of American history as a great inventor of his time. However, the local impact felt by the community in which he lived can be easily obscured by his role as a national figure. Thomas A. Edison Jr. High School, now the Edison Middle School, was dedicated in his honor on October 11, 1929, when it opened, and Edison himself attended opening ceremonies. The local legacy of Edison will forever endure within the minds and hearts of town residents as West Orange's most famous adopted son.

Chapter 7

THEY LEFT THEIR MARK ON US

The Grand Old Man of Football: Amos Alonzo Stagg

The name of Amos Alonzo Stagg might be familiar to town residents because of the playground named in his honor next to the St. Cloud School. However, most might not be aware of his amazing accomplishments in life and his nationally recognized notoriety in college football, baseball, track and basketball. He may be best known as coaching college football for 71 years. But Stagg had a combined total of coaching 125 years in all sports. All his many coaching accomplishments are also easily overshadowed by his spectacular career as a baseball player that begins in the 1880s as a pitcher for Orange High School.

Amos Alonzo Stagg is known as the "Grand Old Man of Football" and was born on August 16, 1862, in West Orange. He died over a century later on March 17, 1965 in Stockton, California. His amazing life spanned over 102 years from the time of President Abraham Lincoln during the Civil War to President Lyndon Johnson when U.S. Marines first landed in Vietnam.

However, from an accurate historical standpoint, Stagg was not born in West Orange. At the date of Stagg's birth, West Orange did not exist. His house was in what was then Orange. On March 11, 1862, an act of the New Jersey legislature created the Township of Fairmount by taking away a section of Orange. It wasn't until April 10, 1863, that another act of the New Jersey legislature created the township of West Orange by combining

The house where Stagg was born on August 16, 1862, is still standing on Valley Road. This image is circa 1875. *Courtesy Robert Stagg.*

all the land of Fairmount Township and another section of Orange to form today's West Orange. Stagg's birthplace at 384 Valley Road was never in the township of Fairmount, but it went from being in Orange to West Orange on April 10, 1863, about eight months after Stagg's birth. If there were birth certificates issued in his day, his place of birth would have been listed as Orange, New Jersey. So Stagg himself is actually older than the town of West Orange itself. However, Stagg always accurately indicated that he grew up in West Orange and always considered it his true hometown. West Orange has always rightfully claimed Stagg as one of its own, and the Stagg homestead where he grew up, built in 1848, is still standing on Valley Road in West Orange today.

Stagg was born into a poor family and was the fifth of eight children. He was raised with stern virtues that followed him his whole life. Fortitude, self-reliance and discipline became part of his personality at a young age. He began working as a laborer, which he did willingly and cheerfully. Stagg's mother had died while he was still a child, and he soon became acutely aware of his father's struggles to support the family and recognized the need for higher education. In his day,

Stagg pictured as a young man in an undated photograph. *Courtesy Robert Stagg.*

however, a high school diploma was a goal that few achieved. In 1878, Stagg joined the First Presbyterian Church of Orange and became further influenced by both education and religion. As a youngster growing up in West Orange, Stagg often swam and ice-skated on a small pond known as Cook's Pond, where Edison's laboratories were eventually built on Main Street in 1887, then known as Valley Road.

Stagg later enrolled in Orange High School (because West Orange did not have one of its own at the time), and he had to pay a tuition fee. He participated in athletics and gained notoriety as a star pitcher for the high school baseball team. The combined elements of a strong body and mind helped mold his moral character. He graduated from Orange High School in 1883 and, despite financial struggles, went on to college.

In 1884, he enrolled in Yale as a divinity student. It was here that he really excelled in baseball. He pitched Yale University to five straight baseball championships from 1886 to 1890. He turned down a $4,200 contract following graduation to play professional baseball for the New York Nationals. He did so because he believed a college man should be able to make money at a real job. He also called into question the character of professional baseball since alcohol, which he despised and never used, was sold at games. A baseball game program from the Orange Athletic Club reveals that Stagg was also a pitcher for their baseball team. The program indicates that on October 6, 1888, he pitched against the Staten Island Athletic Club. The game was held at the Orange Oval on Grove Street in East Orange, which was the home field of the Orange Athletic Club despite being in East Orange.

Stagg started playing football in 1886 for Yale, and the following year, he was selected to Walter Camp's first All-American football team. After college, he

Stagg is seated to the extreme left and pictured with the Yale football team of 1888. *Courtesy Robert Stagg.*

began his legendary football coaching career that spanned seventy-one years. He was elected to the College Football Hall of Fame as both a player and a coach in the charter class of 1951. Stagg had a great impact on the game by aiding in the development of many of the basic tactics that are still used to this day. They include the forward pass, the man in motion, the T formation and the lateral pass. Knute Rockne, the famous football coach of Notre Dame, was once asked how he thought up his football plays. Rockne responded by saying, "I get them from Stagg, and Stagg gets them from God."

The inventor of the game of basketball in 1892 was James Naismith. But Naismith was an early football teammate of Stagg's, and in fact, it was Stagg's suggestion to Naismith that made the sport of basketball five players to a side as we know it today. Stagg also played in the first-ever public basketball game at the Springfield, Massachusetts YMCA on March 11, 1892. He scored the only basket as the faculty lost to the students, 5–1. Stagg was elected to the College Basketball Hall of Fame in its first group of inductees in 1959.

In 1900, Stagg served as a track and field coach with the United States Olympic team at the summer Olympics in Paris. Before embarking, he wrote a touching and revealing letter to his fourteen-month-old son. Stagg wanted to ensure that his infant son would know how to live his life if somehow Stagg did not survive the Atlantic crossing to Europe. The timeless advice of the letter read, in part, "Your father wants you to detest evil. No curiosity, no conversation, no story, no reading which suggests impurity of life is worthy of your thought and I beg you never to yield for an instant but turn your attention to something good and helpful. Never use liquors, tobacco, nor profane language."

Shortly before his death in 1965, some kids were playing football on Stagg's front lawn in Stockton, California. A concerned neighbor noticed and quietly approached Stagg to inform him that his grass would never grow that way. Stagg smiled and just politely replied, "I'm not trying to grow grass; I'm trying to grow kids."

A thirteen-acre West Orange playground in the St. Cloud section of West Orange was named Stagg Field at dedication ceremonies on Saturday, May 8, 1954, and will turn fifty years old in 2014. Stagg himself was unable to come but sent his son Amos Alonzo Stagg Jr. Mayor Fred Erwin, Director of Parks and Public Property Frank Moran and West Orange commissioners Charles Neil and Edward Roos were there among those representing the town in the large crowd present.

During the West Orange Sesquicentennial Celebration in 2012, the following congratulatory remarks were sent by Amos Alonzo Stagg III, the grandson of the legendary coach: "We congratulate West Orange during the year of your 150th Anniversary. Your community has much to be proud of. We hope that one of our family members can return to West Orange in the near future to revisit the house built in 1848 where Amos Alonzo Stagg was born in 1862."

Robert Stagg, with whom I made contact to request the family statement, is Amos Alonzo Stagg's great-grandson. Coincidentally, since my great-grandfather Richard Fagan was born in Orange just a few years after Stagg, both our great-grandfathers likely attended school together in Orange, since all grades went to the same school building.

The state of New Jersey enacted a new law in 1892 requiring all townships to establish a local board of education. The first president of the newly formed West Orange Board of Education was George R. Stagg, Amos's older brother. George was born on October 26, 1850, in the same house in West Orange as his famous younger brother. George Stagg served as first president of the West Orange school board from 1892 to 1897. Prior to becoming president, he had labored for more than fifteen years as an advocate

Right: George Stagg was the first president of the newly formed West Orange Board of Education in 1892. *Author's collection.*

Below: Town clerk Thurman Williams is seen bringing official greeting from Mayor James Sheeran to Stagg in 1962. *Courtesy Robert Williams.*

for children who were dependent on the public schools for their education. George acquired his education in the public schools of Orange, just like Amos, but supplemented his schooling with private study and extensive reading. George Stagg's contributions may have been overshadowed by his younger brother, but they played an important role and helped set the successful course for West Orange education.

The sisters of Amos Alonzo Stagg continued to live at his childhood home in West Orange into the 1950s. Amos visited them often, but his last visit to West Orange was in 1947.

When he turned one hundred years old in 1962, the town clerk of West Orange, Thurman Williams, brought official greeting from West Orange mayor James Sheeran. Williams happened to be attending a convention in California near the nursing home where Stagg was confined at the time. When Stagg passed away at 102 years of age on March 17, 1965, Mayor Sheeran decreed that all flags in West Orange be flown at half mast for a one-week period as a final West Orange tribute. Stagg will forever be remembered fondly as one of West Orange's native sons who always adhered to the fundamentals of good living and did so by setting a good example for all others to follow.

Cast a Long Shadow: Brian Piccolo

One of the most inspiring stories of personal struggles in NFL history has a little-known West Orange connection. In 1964, during his senior season at Wake Forest, Brian Piccolo led the nation in rushing and scoring. In the world of college football, Piccolo was a virtual unknown, but he maintained high hopes for the NFL draft. Much to his disappointment, he was not selected by any team. Despite his success in college football, he was considered too small and slow to be a professional running back in the NFL. George Halas, owner of the Chicago Bears, however, believed in Piccolo's potential and signed him as a free agent in 1965.

At that time, my father and uncle operated a gas station known as Fagan's Texaco on the corner of Northfield Avenue and Old Short Hills Road, just over the West Orange border. It was down the street from the newly completed St. Barnabas Hospital in Livingston. DeCamp Bus Lines stopped in front of the service station on Northfield Avenue to drop off hospital visitors and employees, but they had to walk almost a mile up the hill to reach the hospital. The management of St. Barnabas quickly realized this

Brian Piccolo as a young boy in June 1954, taken where he grew up in Florida. *Courtesy Don Piccolo.*

problem and alleviated the hardship by providing a jitney bus service that would stop at Fagan's Texaco and park on the corner in between runs.

The first driver of the jitney bus was Joe Piccolo. His son Brian had just signed with the Chicago Bears. Joe would wait inside the office of the gas station, and my father and uncle quickly got to know him pretty well. His son Brian signing with the Chicago Bears was naturally an interesting topic for conversation. Joe Piccolo and his wife had recently moved up to New Jersey from their home in Florida. They lived in the West Mill Apartments in West Orange on Old Short Hills Road across from St. Barnabas Hospital. They came to New Jersey for the purpose of working in a family business in nearby Paterson. The stress of the move and new business venture, however, caused Joe unexpected health problems that landed him in the hospital at St. Barnabas. While hospitalized and recovering, he was offered a less stressful job as driver for the new jitney bus service. Upon being discharged from the hospital, he took the job and began driving the bus.

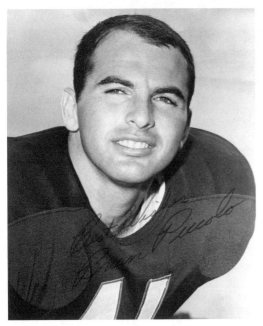

Above: Fagan's Texaco Service much as it looked when Joe Piccolo parked the jitney bus he was driving on the corner. *Author's collection.*

Left: Autographed picture received by Joseph Fagan and sent directly from Brian Piccolo in 1965. *Author's collection.*

I was just nine years old, and my father asked Joe Piccolo to have his son Brian send me an autographed picture. Shortly after, I received an unexpected envelope in the mail containing a signed picture of Brian Piccolo from the Chicago Bears. I had never heard of Piccolo or the Bears before, but the picture immediately cast a spell on me. My father and I instantly became Chicago Bear fans from that day forward, closely following Piccolo's career. Joe Piccolo continued driving the bus for a short time but one day mysteriously disappeared. He was replaced as the bus driver, and my father and uncle never knew why or saw him again.

Years later, I had posted the story about the West Orange connection in an online blog. A short time afterward, I received a phone call from Brian's older brother Don Piccolo. Don explained to me that many inaccurate statements have been written about his brother Brian, but when he read my story, he felt compelled to call me because no one else ever knew these details about his parents in West Orange. Don further shared with me the story about why his father disappeared from New Jersey. Joe Piccolo had received a call in the middle of the night from his neighbor in Florida informing him that his hot water heater had sprung a leak. Joe was so disturbed over the alarming news that he and his wife loaded up the car in the middle of the night, fled West Orange and returned home to Florida without telling anyone.

As a running back in the NFL, Brian Piccolo had more determination than skill and was primarily used as a backup player. His biggest competition was a number-one draft pick by the Chicago Bears named Gale Sayers. Sayers would become an NFL star and future hall of famer. Piccolo finally got his chance to play in 1969 after several injuries to key players, including Sayers, but a problem developed. Brian discovered a tumor in his chest that was subsequently diagnosed as embryonal cell carcinoma, which eventually tested positive for cancer. Brian Piccolo bravely fought the disease to the end but sadly passed away on June 16, 1970, at the age of twenty-six. His courageous fight with cancer inspired the 1971 TV movie *Brian's Song*, starring James Caan, Billy Dee Williams and several of Brian's teammates.

At the time of his diagnosis in 1970, embryonal cell carcinoma was nearly 100 percent fatal because little was known about it. After Piccolo's death, the Brian Piccolo Cancer Research Fund was established. Since then, millions of dollars have been raised for research on various forms of this disease. Piccolo's saga made national news and raised considerable awareness, saving countless lives. Today, with early detection and treatment, this type of cancer is now almost completely curable.

Brian Piccolo became an NFL icon and legend but not for his accomplishments on the football field. My father first met Joe Piccolo in West Orange when he drove people to the hospital. Ironically, the research inspired by the tragic death of his youngest son may have driven thousands more away from the hospital. Many have been saved thanks to Brian's remarkable courage and determination. His enduring legacy casts a long shadow, even reaching West Orange, where his parents briefly lived, in a way he never could have imagined.

Sink or Swim Brings Olympic Glory

Amateur athletes spend years preparing and waiting to realize their dream for the opportunity to capture Olympic glory. A young West Orange girl realized one such dream as she stepped on to the world stage at the 1964 Tokyo Summer Olympics and won two Olympic medals. Virginia "Ginny" Duenkel was only seventeen years old and a student at West Orange High School when she won both a gold and bronze medal in swimming competitions. However, Ginny revealed to me in an interview that this most memorable moment in her life almost never happened.

The Duenkel family lived at 117 Fairview Avenue in West Orange, and by age nine, Ginny and her two brothers, along with their parents, were spending summers at the St. Cloud Swim Club. The club was once located on Pleasant Valley Way near Northfield Avenue. Ginny was always afraid of the pool and entertained herself by just hanging out and was completely happy avoiding the water. That all changed in 1956 when Ginny's father, frustrated by her lack of interest, suddenly tossed her into the shallow end of the pool. It caused quite a stir with a lot of yelling and screaming, but Ginny quickly realized the water was only knee deep. She soon grew comfortable with the idea of actually being in the pool and gradually learned to swim.

In a short time, it became apparent that Ginny had a natural talent for swimming that had long been concealed by her fear of the water. She then joined the swim team at St. Cloud, and her coach, Frank Elm, was the first to realize Ginny's true potential. He taught her discipline and helped develop her natural ability into refined techniques. Under Elm's guidance, Ginny became a contender with a strong work ethic. She soon learned that the more she achieved, the more she believed in herself and began to set goals for herself. Her first major test came at the 1963 Pan American Games in São Paulo, Brazil. There she won a gold medal and established a world record for the one-hundred-meter backstroke. A year later, she found herself at the 1964 Summer Olympics in Tokyo, Japan, with the same goal in mind. Ginny recounted for me how going into the '64 Olympics, she really expected to win a gold medal for the one-hundred-meter backstroke since she was the world record holder. Instead, she came in third and won the bronze. She was devastated by her inability to capture gold. When the bronze medal was placed around her neck on the victory stand, she was crying. They were not tears of joy, as most would have expected; instead, she was crying about not winning the gold.

Ginny Duenkel is seen holding flowers entering Colgate Field following a parade on Ginny Duenkel Day in West Orange on November 15, 1964. *Author's collection.*

Ginny had also qualified for the four-hundred-meter freestyle at the 1964 Olympics and had two days to prepare for the event. Her coach told Ginny that every swimmer there, including herself, was in top physical condition and that the key to winning was just in the mental preparation. Ginny quickly grasped that concept and used it to her advantage. She closed her eyes and visualized the race going on while going over every move and turn in her mind. Ginny explained to me with amazing emotion even some forty-five years later how she profoundly knew at the start of that race even before hitting the water that she would win because she was totally prepared mentally. This time, when they hung the gold medal around her neck, she was crying tears of pure joy. She had not yet graduated from West Orange High School but amazingly had won two Olympic medals and set a new Olympic record in the four-hundred-meter freestyle of 4:43.3. If Ginny's father had not tossed her in the pool to sink or swim and overcome her fear of water on that summer day in 1956, her potential may have never been known to the world.

After the Olympics, Ginny returned as a hometown hero, and November 15, 1964, was declared Ginny Duenkel Day in West Orange. A parade was held on Main Street in her honor with an estimated crowd of twelve

Ginny is standing at the ladder with hometown kids on the first Ginny Duenkel Day at the town pool during the summer of 1967. *Courtesy West Orange Recreation Department.*

thousand in attendance. She said it was surreal to have lived a dream and accomplish her goals. After high school, Ginny briefly attended college to study nursing. There she met her husband, Chris Fuldner, before moving to Denver. After a few years of marriage, they relocated from Denver to Monett, Missouri, in 1977 to work in the Fuldner family business. They still live there, where they have raised two daughters and a son and now have three grandsons. In 1989, Ginny started a swim team named the Water Thrashers in Monett with 12 swimmers, though that number has since grown to over 125.

On June 2, 1967, the West Orange Recreation Department opened a new town swimming pool named the Ginny Duenkel Pool. It remains today in recognition of her Olympic achievements. Ginny has dear memories of West Orange and, despite living out of state, still considers it her hometown. West Orange will always fondly remember her as the hometown girl who brought home Olympic gold.

The Railroad Tycoon of West Orange: Leonor Loree

Anyone traveling up the sharp steep curve on Mt. Pleasant Avenue above Gregory Avenue surely has noticed the stone masonry walls that border the road on the left. They almost seem to have been part of some mysterious fortress guarding the Prospect Avenue intersection. But the only thing the walls protect is a well-concealed history.

The walls bordering the Loree estate and Mt. Pleasant Avenue are seen shortly after constructed in 1917. *Author's collection.*

In the 1890s, the property on this corner was owned by Treadwell Cleveland, a prominent New York attorney. His second cousin Stephen, better known as Grover Cleveland, was then serving as the president of the United States. Tredwell Cleveland's Orange Mountain home sat above a cliff overlooking the former O'Rourke's Quarry directly below. The quarry was a geological curiosity in the 1870s because of distinctive columnar rock formations discovered there and still visible today resembling the Giant's Causeway in Ireland.

Before Cleveland passed away, Leonor Loree, a railroad executive, became Cleveland's neighbor about 1912 on adjoining property to the south. However, unlike Cleveland, Loree made West Orange his principal place of residence. Loree graduated from Rutgers in 1877 and went on to become president of five major railroads at various times. Loree also played a pivotal role in the creation of the New Jersey College for Women, later Douglass College and now known as Douglass Residential College. At the outbreak of World War I in 1914, Americans, including Loree, traveling in Europe were cut off from safe passage home. Loree arranged to charter the Southern Pacific steamship *Antilles* to bring home 252 stranded Americans. In 1925, Loree helped built an athletic field at Rutgers, still in existence, named Antilles Field after the ship that had brought him and the other stranded Americans safely home.

When Treadwell Cleveland passed away in 1918, Loree purchased the neighboring property. Loree went on to built a sprawling estate that included a twenty-seven-room mansion with eight bathrooms known as Bowood. The current Ridge Road off Mt. Pleasant Avenue crossed his property totaling thirty-one acres that also included a second residence containing thirteen rooms and five bathrooms.

Other amenities on the Loree estate included a recreation house, tennis courts and various garages, as well as farm buildings, including stables for both riding horses and polo ponies with a four-hundred-foot exercise track. There was also a cow barn, chicken houses, feed and supply sheds, a caretaker's cottage and a greenhouse. Loree built the stone masonry walls surrounding his estate in 1917, and they still border Mt. Pleasant and

Opposite, top: A real estate drawing of the grounds of the Loree estate, circa 1940 *Author's collection.*

Opposite, bottom: The main house of the Loree estate is seen circa 1935. *Author's collection.*

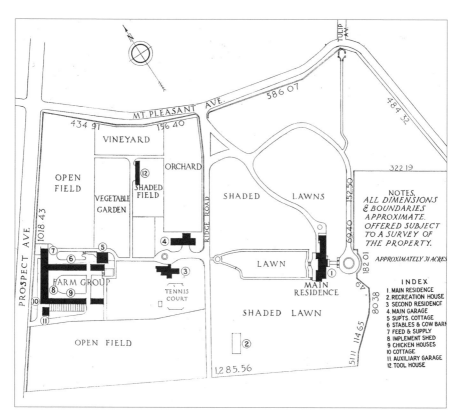

Prospect Avenues today. The construction cost of the walls was reported in excess of $60,000.

Many members of the Loree family eventually lived at Bowood, including Lenor Loree's daughter Louise Claire and her husband, Dave Collins, and Loree's three grandsons. During the 1930s, Loree's son-in-law Dave Collins realized that his two oldest sons—Dave, better known as "Rip," and Tabor—were living a leisurely life that lacked an important virtue. Dave felt his sons needed to learn mental toughness in order to achieve future success like their grandfather. He thought that this could best be accomplished by exposing his sons to the rugged kids he observed on the playground at West Orange's Colgate Field. Collins conceived the idea to form a football team for his sons and the twelve- to thirteen-year-old boys from down the hill. Thus a team was born: the Colgate Tigers, who played on a regulation-size football field built on the Loree estate. Collins outfitted the team with full equipment and uniforms, including blue and gold numbered jerseys. Games were complete with first down markers, player benches, goal posts and referees. Spectators were often invited guests of Dave Collins and were given food and drink provided by the Bowood staff. Collins also arranged for a full eight- or nine-game season with opposition against private schools, such as Kingsley Prep, Montclair Athletic Club, Bonnie Brae School and other local teams.

Dave Collins would send two chauffeur-driven station wagons down to Colgate Field to gather the boys. From there, they would be transported only a short physical distance to the private grounds of the football field on the Loree estate. But in terms of lifestyle and background, the distance for the local boys was worlds apart from that of the Collins boys. It was a welcomed distraction for the youngsters from the many hardships their families often endured during the Depression.

Upon arrival, the boys were directed into a barn that served as a locker room to change into their uniforms. When the game ended, the boys would change back into their street clothes, but Dave Collins generously allowed the boys to spend the rest of the day roaming the grounds. They were also provided with meals prepared by the Bowood staff. Dave Collins was known to encouraged the local boys to pick fights with his son Rip in order to toughen him up. The strategy apparently proved successful since Rip advanced to a college football career at Annapolis. His other son, Dave, was also chosen as Most Valuable Player at the Sun Bowl years later.

For the boys from down the hill, the games offered an opportunity for supervised football during the Depression that they otherwise might not have had. The diverse backgrounds of the Collins boys and the playground

Undated photo circa 1930s of the Colgate Tigers football team organized by Dave Collins with kids from down the hill. *Courtesy John Healy.*

kids provided a means by which they each could teach and learn from one another. Learning self-confidence that only competition among peers can teach helped them all achieve future success.

Leonor Loree passed away peacefully at his West Orange estate on September 6, 1940, at age eighty-two. Shortly following his death in 1940, the newly constructed Carteret School opened on five acres in West Orange on Prospect Avenue, about a mile south of the Loree estate. In 1943, the Carteret School acquired all the property and buildings of the Loree estate. The former stately Loree mansion was converted into school dormitories and renamed Loree Hall. All the other buildings were also transformed for school use into additional dormitories, staff buildings, recreation areas, a day camp and, at one time, a nursery school. The Carteret School closed in 1970, and the building was demolished in the 1990s. Only the school's former gymnasium survives today as part of the current Seton Hall Prep Athletic Complex. The former Loree estate and other buildings last owned by the Carteret School were all eventually torn down.

I have acquired boxes of items, documents and photos that all once belonged to the former Carteret School. Included in this collection are real estate brochures, magazine articles, detailed drawings of the grounds and many rare photographs, all of the former Loree buildings. They perhaps are the only surviving record giving testimony to the once magnificent beauty of the former grounds. These photos provide an unprecedented glimpse into how life once existed on the other side of the walls for both Loree and the Carteret School. Today, the stone walls peek out from some overgrown ivy, quietly blending into the suburban landscape as a timeless monument now only protecting a lost memory.

The Killing Fields of Cambodia Come to Eagle Rock

As the tragic events unfolded on September 11, 2001, the Eagle Rock Reservation in West Orange stood in stunned silence while a horrified nation watched. On that dreadful day, our nation's resolve was tested but not defeated, and our spirit was badly bruised but not broken. A permanent memorial now stands at Eagle Rock and honors all those who perished on that fateful day.

During the summer of 2002, construction was well underway for the Eagle Rock September 11 Memorial. It was not yet completed but on schedule for dedication ceremonies on October 20, 2002. I had been making regular trips to Eagle Rock all that summer to document the construction and subsequently have nearly one thousand pictures archived of the changes that took place during construction. For the Memorial Day weekend of 2002, rain was in the forecast, and gray cloudy skies had put the feel of a slight early autumn chill in the air. Despite the unpromising nature of the weather, I decided to go to Eagle Rock to check on the construction progress and take a few more pictures. Upon arriving, I was not surprised to find the park completely empty, but on this day, I somehow sensed something would be different.

I soon became oblivious to my surroundings as I was taking pictures. Suddenly, I bumped into another person who was also taking pictures there. He seemed to emerge from the shadows, and I was startled and momentarily stunned by his quiet presence. We were the only two at Eagle Rock, and his camera—unlike mine—suggested that he might be a professional photographer. He confirmed my suspicions when he told me that he was a newspaper photographer who had been sent to take pictures. Our chance meeting was polite and cordial, and we engaged in conversation for only a few minutes.

Dith Pran is seen taking photos at the Eagle Rock Reservation on October 20, 2002. *Author's collection.*

He told me that he had worked for the *New York Times* for the last thirty years and that he had also covered the Vietnam War for the same newspaper. He was an elderly man of Asian descent, which piqued my curiosity. He told me that he was from Cambodia and explained how the people of Cambodia suffered after the war under Pol Pot, the leader of the Khmer Rouge. I told him that I was aware of the history and had learned about it from the movie *The Killing Fields*. He just smiled and seemed very pleased that I knew what he was talking about. He paused for a second, looked me in the eye and then proudly stated in a soft-spoken, gentle voice, "That movie was made about my life."

At that point, I suddenly realized to whom I was speaking. The friendly man I just befriended was Dith Pran, the photo journalist from the *New York Times* whose heroic story was portrayed in the 1984 movie *The Killing Fields*. We instantly connected and spent the next five hours talking. He personally recounted for me his experiences in Vietnam and Cambodia and his four years of torture and starvation by the Khmer Rouge before his escape to Thailand. I listened, I learned and I asked why. There was not a good answer.

Dith Pran meeting my son, Joseph Fagan, at a Hopatcong High School assembly in 2005. *Author's collection.*

I learned there never will be a good answer. Dith Pran personally taught me about the best and the worst of mankind.

I remained friendly with Dith Pran following our chance encounter. I even had the opportunity to introduce him to my son Joseph when we last met when he visited his high school to give a speech in 2005.

The last e-mail Dith Pran sent me was in December 2007 and is still on my computer. Sadly, only three months later, Dith Pran passed away of pancreatic cancer on March 30, 2008. The 1984 movie *The Killing Fields* chronicling his epic saga won three Academy awards and is worth watching to better understand our freedom and liberty. The Khmer Rouge imprisoned, tortured and starved him, but they couldn't break him. Despite his anguish and circumstances, his will to survive endured. I believe Dith Pran is one of history's chosen messengers, and he taught me that to forget the atrocities of the past is even worse than the atrocities themselves. From him, I personally learned of the violent killing fields of Cambodia right on the peaceful fields of West Orange's Eagle Rock.

The Last Surviving Slave of Essex County

Just like Dith Pran's epic struggle for freedom from enslavement, our own American history has a similar story of a people's long struggle for freedom. One town resident was an African American whose life has been long overlooked. He lived during a period in American history when prejudice and social injustice controlled his fate. Despite being born into slavery, he became a free man and was the last surviving slave of Essex County and lived in West Orange.

Anthony Thompson was born into slavery in Somerset County, New Jersey, in 1798. His great-grandmother, whom he never knew, was reported to have been the queen of an African tribe. His mother was taken away from the tribe at a young age and brought to America by an African slave trader. By 1798, she was enslaved and property of the family of Reverend Philip Duryee of the Dutch Reformed Church in Raritan when Anthony was born. By subsequent sales, both Anthony and his mother became the property of Samuel M. Ward of what was then known as Cranetown and today is Montclair, New Jersey. When Ward died in 1822, he left in his will that Anthony should be given his freedom. Ward also left a small amount of money to Anthony to help him make a life for himself as a free man.

Anthony was just twenty-four at the time he was given his freedom, and his mother had previously been freed before Mr. Ward's death. Anthony's mother, however, was incapable of making a life for herself, mostly due to the limitations of her old age. It was the custom at that time to sell the poor who were dependent on public charity to the highest bidder. As a free man, Anthony sadly purchased his own mother at public auction for $100 and cared for her until her death.

As a freed man, Anthony began working for Benjamin Williams at Tory Corner in what today is West Orange. (Benjamin Williams is also mentioned in Chapter 1.) Williams was a prominent man of the Orange area whose family was among the original settlers. Thompson was able to make a living over the years by working for five generations of the Williams family. Anthony Thompson eventually purchased a small home that once stood at the present-day corner of Main and Washington Streets at Tory Corner in West Orange. Anthony was reported to have obtained a fair education, which likely meant that he learned to read and write. He was married twice but never had any children.

The life of a slave certainly was a dreadful existence during a dismal era in this nation's history. It robbed individuals of their personal identities and freedoms. It also inflicted deep emotional pain by separating many families forever. When examined through the prism of the twenty-first century, it may be difficult to understand how such a tradition was permitted to exist by a nation founded on Christian-Judaea beliefs. The American Civil War (1861–65) was fought mainly based on the sovereignty of states' rights, but the issue of slavery was arguably the principal catalyst. The entire Southern economy at the time was completely dependent on slave labor. Interestingly, however, New Jersey was the last Northern state to abolish slavery. It began gradually in 1804, when children of slaves were first considered to be born free.

Despite the indignity of once being enslaved, Thompson stated in 1882 that most, but not all, slaves in New Jersey had kind masters and that he himself had never witnessed a slave beaten. Certainly, he would have known prejudice in his day, but by most accounts, he was well liked and lived a peaceful existence as a free man since 1822. He likely never experienced the evil brutality of slavery as it once existed in the Deep South, and he was well thought of in West Orange by several accounts.

In later years, he was affectionately known as "Uncle Anthony." He recalled that he could remember when all the land in West Orange between the first mountain and Newark was a sprawling wilderness. Nearly all the land at that time was owned by the Harrison, Dodd and Williams families, who all belonged to the First Presbyterian Church in Orange. Thompson and other former slaves also were members there but sat in an area of the church separate from the white settlers.

Uncle Anthony Thompson passed away peacefully at age eighty-six on Tuesday, September 16, 1884, at his West Orange home, leaving behind a second wife. Although born into slavery, Thompson overcame the social injustice of his day and proudly died a free man. His forgotten legacy is often overlooked, despite his being the last surviving slave of Essex County who lived in West Orange. Remembering his life today pays tribute to him and all those who have struggled to enact social change in the name of equality.

Chapter 8

GENERAL GEORGE McCLELLAN

The Untold West Orange Story

One prominent West Orange resident played a major role in this nation's Civil War and nearly changed the entire course of American history. General George McClellan first arrived in West Orange while still on active duty. He had been relieved of his command by President Lincoln for his failure to pursue Confederate general Robert E. Lee shortly following the Battle of Antietam on September 17, 1862. McClellan was then officially reassigned to Trenton, New Jersey, with no clear understanding of his future role in the war.

Circumstances and not personal choice most likely dictated why McClellan decided to come to West Orange. His father-in-law, U.S. Army general Randolph Marcy, had already established roots in West Orange. Randolph Marcy's elder brother Dr. E.E. Marcy was a prominent and successful New York City homeopathic doctor who first came to West Orange about 1859 when it was still part of Orange. Dr. Marcy had purchased two hundred acres of rugged woodland along the mountain ridge on the top of the first mountain, cleared the land and built several home sites. By 1863, Dr. Marcy, McClellan's wife's uncle, had a home along the ridge on the first mountain in West Orange.

By January 1863, McClellan and his family took up residence at a Fifth Avenue hotel in New York City. McClellan was soon presented with a gift from loyal supporters of a fully furnished four-story brick town house on West Thirty-first Street in Manhattan, to which he and his family removed. However, by the spring of 1863, New York City was overcome with violent draft riots. The overall atmosphere steadily deteriorated, becoming unstable and dangerous. McClellan likely decided to seek seclusion and safety for his family in the Orange Mountains because his wife's father and uncle already had homes there.

McClellan's train arrived in Orange promptly at 3:30 p.m. on Saturday, June 27, 1863, one week before the Battle of Gettysburg, to join his wife and daughter, who had come only days earlier. Excited crowds had gathered in jubilant anticipation to welcome the beloved and famous general. McClellan emerged onto the train station platform in civilian dress among resounding cheers of well-wishers. He made a few briefs remarks before being driven away in a carriage to the mountain ridge home of Dr. Marcy, where he would temporarily reside with his family. He was still on active army duty and was expecting to receive further orders from President Lincoln, but orders never came.

Left to right, top: Dr. Marcy, George McClellan, Mrs. McClellan (wife) and Mrs. Marcy; *bottom*: George McClellan Jr. (son), Emma Marcy and Mary "May" McClellan (daughter) in West Orange circa 1874. *Author's collection.*

The general's West Orange home, named Maywood after his daughter, much as it looked in the 1870s. *Author's collection.*

McClellan quickly appreciated the peaceful surroundings of the mountain ridge in West Orange. He eventually built his own home here and named it Maywood after his daughter. He maintained a home in New York City and lived abroad but established deep and enduring roots in the West Orange community. McClellan built his own home in West Orange about 1870, and a map from 1872 shows Dr. Marcy, his brother General Randolph Marcy (McClellan's father-in-law) and McClellan as neighbors along the ridge.

On August 31, 1864, McClellan won the nomination of the Democratic Party to oppose Abraham Lincoln in the presidential election of 1864. A big reception was held in West Orange that night to celebrate McClellan's pending presidential bid against Lincoln. The campaign was primarily conducted by the Democratic Party, as was the custom at that time, while McClellan remained mostly in seclusion in West Orange. It was considered at that time to be a sign of weakness if a candidate was seen in public. The campaign began only two months before the election—not two years before, like campaigns do today. McClellan was optimistic for a victory but lost in a landslide. Had he won, the course of the Civil War and American history as we know it might have changed.

The Democrats were in favor of negotiating with the Confederacy to bring an immediate end the war. Although McClellan didn't agree fully with this position, our country easily could have been divided into two separate nations under a McClellan presidency if he had been pressured to follow the party platform. The day following his loss to Lincoln, McClellan wrote a very profound letter from West Orange to his mother in Philadelphia, describing how relieved he was that the responsibility of reuniting the nation would not fall on his shoulders. Disappointed by his defeat to Lincoln, McClellan left for Europe with his family and didn't return to West Orange until after the end of the Civil War.

At the time of the election in 1864, the technology had not yet been developed to put actual photographs in the newspaper like we do today. Etchings or drawings of individuals were used instead. An artist would etch a reverse drawing onto a copper or zinc plate mounted on a wooden print block that ink could be applied to in a printing press to provide an image of the person. Some years ago, I purchased a print block bearing the image of George McClellan that was widely used during his national campaign in many newspapers. I can actually date it to 1861 when it was first used by a group of local supporters known as the McClellan Society in a Newark, New Jersey newspaper. It survives as a genuine one-of-a-kind national McClellan artifact also used during the election of 1864 and connects to West Orange, where he lived at the time. Campaign ads in 1864 only showed the candidate's home state and not usually the town where he lived. McClellan was listed as being from New Jersey, and his hometown of West Orange was not mentioned.

To this day, certain facts concerning the death of Civil War general George McClellan in West Orange have otherwise been lost to history and never before reported. Most history books and countless Internet resources all state that Civil War general George McClellan passed away on October 29, 1885, in Orange, New Jersey. Although this date is correct, the location is unequivocally and absolutely wrong. This error has long been perpetuated by even the most expert of McClellan scholars, who do not realize that Orange and West Orange are two separate places. This misunderstanding likely began simply because West Orange did not have its own post office. Even today with modern zip codes, West Orange is still only a branch of the neighboring Orange post office. All of McClellan's mail and other correspondence were addressed to Orange. Even though McClellan knew that his home was in West Orange, the rest of the world only knew it as Orange.

Local newspaper accounts of his death accurately list the place of his death—specifically, at his home of Maywood in West Orange. But these

A side-by-side comparison of the print block used to make newspaper impressions of George McClellan during the election of 1864. *Author's collection.*

newspaper accounts are rarely seen and only available by painstakingly searching through outdated microfilm. However, a firsthand account that survives only by word of mouth will not be found in any newspaper or history book. The actual story has been passed on to me by someone who was told it directly from someone present at McClellan's 1885 death. Perhaps seen here for the first time in print, it will set the record straight about how the rest of the world first learned of his death.

McClellan had been on a trip west with his father-in-law and neighbor, General Randolph Marcy, in August 1885. McClellan's custom was to quietly remember each anniversary of the battle of Antietam every September at Maywood in West Orange. McClellan and Marcy therefore returned home by September 17, 1885, to reflect on the bloodiest battle in American history only twenty-three years earlier, in which McClellan had been the Union army commander. Shortly afterward, in early October, McClellan began to experience severe chest pains. His doctor, Dr. Steward of Orange, diagnosed it as angina pectoris likely caused from stress on his recent trip. McClellan was prescribed bed rest. Within a few weeks, he started feeling better, and it seemed a complete recovery was possible. McClellan soon resorted to riding his horse named Daniel Webster around West Orange. The same horse had served him well at the battle of Antietam and came to Maywood with McClellan, and the horse is still in West Orange because it was buried on McClellan's former property.

By October 28, 1885, the severe chest pains had returned. His situation worsened, and Dr. Steward was summoned. Also at this time, McClellan's neighbor John Crosby Brown (see Chapter 1) had become aware of his failing health, and word had reached New York City about McClellan's potential demise. John Crosby Brown made arrangements with the *New York Sun* newspaper that it could be the first to print the story if McClellan passed in West Orange. It was prearranged that if McClellan died, the flag at Brown's home, Brighthurst, next door to McClellan's, would be lowered to half staff. Thus, the Orange telegraph office would see this signal from the valley below from a telescope and wire word to the *New York Sun* newspaper for the scoop. However, once it became dark, the flag could no longer be seen. It was then determined that an illuminating signal that could be seen at night would have to be sent. It was decided that this could be done from the high tower from Brown's home of Brighthurst above the valley.

About 3:00 a.m. on October 29, 1885, McClellan was sitting in his library at Maywood. The general looked in the direction of his wife and whispered to his doctor, "Tell her I am better now, thank you."

A few moments later, George McClellan passed away at age fifty-eight. According to newspaper reports, among those present with McClellan's wife and daughter was his neighbor John Crosby Brown. Brown's youngest son, Thatcher Brown, age nine, was quickly awakened and hoisted to the top of the narrow tower at Brighthurst. From there, Thatcher sent the illuminating signal proclaiming the beloved general's death to the Orange telegraph office, which in turn wired it on to the *New York Sun* newspaper.

In July 2010, I flew out to St. Louis to interview former West Orange resident Dorothy Robertson. She was born in 1912 on the former McClellan property, where she lived with her family when it was owned by the Delano family and her father was the caretaker. Dorothy was ninety-eight years old at the time of our interview but recalled for me in vivid detail the entire story. In the 1920s, Thatcher Brown (1876–1954) personally told the story about the night McClellan died to the church congregation of the St. Cloud Presbyterian Church in West Orange when Dorothy was a young girl. She explained to me how the story always left a lasting impression on her.

The word of McClellan's death quickly spread across the world. He briefly lay in state at Maywood, where mourners paid their respects. On November

The home of John Crosby Brown, where his son Thatcher Brown was hoisted into the high tower to send the signal McClellan had passed away. *Author's collection.*

2, 1885, his funeral was held at Madison Square Presbyterian Church in New York City. He is interred at Riverview Cemetery in Trenton, New Jersey. But nearly lost to history is the story of young Thatcher Brown, who signaled the world from West Orange, as fondly remembered by Dorothy Robertson.

In 2010, Dorothy was also the last surviving person to actually have lived in McClellan's former West Orange home, which was razed in 1938. During the winter months, the Delano family would go back to New York City, and Dorothy and her family would move into McClellan's former home. It had remained mostly unaltered from McClellan's day with only minor changes. She shared with me many pictures and also described for me many details about the home's interior.

I had previously searched far and wide for detailed information about Maywood and found that it is just not recorded anywhere to be found. But instead, I discovered a direct connection to someone who actually lived there and had been told the story of McClellan's death on October 29, 1885, in West Orange. I recorded my interview with Dorothy to preserve for posterity the forgotten story of General McClellan's pass into eternity.

Dorothy Robertson as a young girl on the front porch of McClellan's former home with a picture of Thatcher Brown, who told her the story. *Author's collection.*

Following McClellan's death, the branch post office on Valley Road in West Orange was renamed the McClellan branch. This name lasted only a few years, and it is unclear why it was changed. Also, when Roosevelt Jr. High School was built in the 1930s, the name first under consideration for the new school was McClellan, but the name of Theodore Roosevelt was eventually chosen. Since McClellan was a founding member of the St. Cloud Presbyterian Church in West Orange in 1877, he is fondly remembered there. To this day, there is a stained-glass window honoring him. It says, "I have fought the good fight, I have finished my course, I have kept the faith."

The last surviving West Orange resident who actually knew George McClellan was Jane MacKenzie, who was also a founding member of the same church with McClellan and John Crosby Brown. She once lived on the corner of Northfield and Ridgeway Avenues and died in 1942. Historians may still debate McClellan's role in American history but likely will never know the untold story of the night he passed away or his enduring impact on his adopted hometown of West Orange.

Chapter 9

CALL TO DUTY

Where Sonny Goes, History Follows

Elmer "Sonny" Ciamillo was born in 1921 and grew up at 11 Lafayette Street in West Orange. Before World War II, he caddied at the original Hutton Park Essex County Country Club in town, once located on Northfield Avenue. Sonny left caddying in 1942 to enlist in the navy during World War II. Mrs. Josephine Thoms, a member of the country club, gave him a silver pin for good luck belonging to her husband before he left for service. The pin was a golf club clasp about three inches long with the letters P.C.T. on it, standing for Primrose C. Thoms. Perhaps Sonny thought it stood for "please carry this," because he always kept it with him as a good luck charm during the war.

During World War II, the battleship USS *Massachusetts* (BB-59) is credited with firing the first naval shot or specifically the first American sixteen-inch projectile of the war. The first shot came from turret 1 on November 8, 1942, when the ship engaged the Vichy French battleship *Jean Bart* in a gun duel as it approached Casablanca in North Africa. On that day, the *Massachusetts* fired 786 of the 800 rounds it held, expelling 98 percent of its ammunition from its sixteen-inch guns. In the process, it not only sank the *Jean Bart* but also contributed to the sinking of five other enemy ships.

On that fateful day, two West Orange boys, only twenty-one years old, were part of the crew and bore witness to history. One was the late Harry McFadden, who had graduated West Orange High School in 1939. Harry was a friend of my father and served as his best man when my father married my mother in

1955. The other sailor that day was Elmer "Sonny" Ciamillo. Amazingly, he was stationed in turret 1 on the *Massachusetts* and was part of the gun crew that fired that first U.S. Navy shot of World War II.

Following the battle at Casablanca, the *Massachusetts* returned stateside for rearmament and reassignment to the South Pacific. Sonny was hoping to return home to West Orange but instead was assigned shore patrol duty while the ship was at port in Boston. While on shore patrol duty, Sonny was present at the deadly Coconut Grove Nightclub fire on November 28, 1942, which was the deadliest nightclub fire in American history. Sonny personally helped carry many of the bodies from the smoldering ruins of the fire that killed 492 people and was injured himself in the process. Unknown to him at the time, one of the individuals he removed from the nightclub was Buck Jones, a famous movie actor who was on a war bond drive and had once starred with John Wayne. Jones died two days later from his injuries.

When the *Massachusetts* set sail for the South Pacific, Sonny was in the sick bay, recovering from his injuries from the fire. After the *Massachusetts* spent some time in the South Pacific, Sonny volunteered to transfer with some of his shipmates from the battleship *Massachusetts* to the aircraft carrier USS *Midway*.

In early October 1944, the *Midway*'s name was changed to *St. Lo*, and it became part of a large task force known as Taffy 3. At dawn on October 25, 1944, the ships of Taffy 3 became engaged in a fight for their lives against Japanese warships at close range. Before reporting to his battle station on the flight deck, Sonny secured $200 in his locker and hastily stuck a spoon in his pocket from a cup of coffee. Inadvertently, the spoon somehow lodged in his pocket behind the clasp of his lucky golf pin, which he was wearing as he manned the five-inch gun topside. No one was prepared for what would happen next in what has become known as the Battle of Leyte Gulf.

Shortly before 11:00 a.m., Taffy 3 came under a heavy concentrated Japanese aerial attack. Sonny and his crew were firing their five-inch gun from the port side of the *St. Lo*, focusing on Japanese warships only ten thousand yards away and closing in. Suddenly, the first Japanese kamikaze pilot seen by the U.S. Navy during World War II rained terror down on the crew of the *St. Lo*. Anti-aircraft guns failed to stop the enemy plane, and it crashed into the flight deck, erupting into a fireball only yards from Sonny. The plane's bomb penetrated the flight deck, exploding *St. Lo*'s bomb magazine on the hangar deck below. Sonny was blown away by the forceful explosion without a life vest and fell nearly 125 feet into the sea, landing on his back. The spoon and golf pin were his only possessions. A quick-thinking

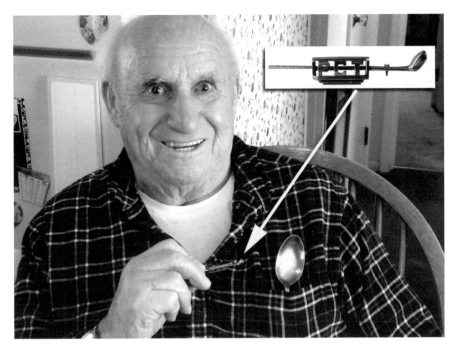

Elmer "Sonny" Ciamillo at his kitchen table in March of 2011 proudly displaying his lucky golf pin and the spoon from the *St. Lo*. *Author's collection.*

U.S. Navy pilot heroically saved Sonny's life when he dropped an inflatable life raft into the water. Injured and dazed from the blast, Sonny likely would have drowned without a life vest. He and several other shipmates were somehow able to reach and inflate the life raft and climb aboard while a fierce naval air and sea battle raged around them. They were surrounded by blazing fires from smoldering oil slicks and could hear the desperate cries of fellow shipmates. They were helpless as they drifted among the dead and injured, and within a half hour, Sonny witnessed the sinking of the *St. Lo*. He then faded in and out of awareness, adrift on the lonely vastness of the Pacific Ocean.

Sonny was eventually plucked out of the Pacific and recovered from his injuries after a long hospital stay. Following the war, he worked for the Town of West Orange for fifty-three and a half years before retiring. The kamikaze attack on the *St. Lo* killed 143 and is considered the first of World War II. Translated into English, kamikaze means "divine wind," but for Sonny on that historic day, the divine wind was trumped by the divine providence of his lucky golf pin, saving him as a witness to history.

West Orange Mayor Escapes the Nazis

A dismal gray autumn sky set the stage for a championship football game. But more adequately, it captured the national sentiment of an uncertain future during the early days of World War II. Any football game could only offer a temporary reprieve for West Orange residents from the headlines of developing world events. Two opposing high school players briefly crossed paths, each in his own way becoming destined to win battles for the betterment of humanity.

In 1942, West Orange was facing Paterson East Side High School. Hope of winning seemed to fade for West Orange just as the blustery winds of war engulfed the world. Larry Doby, the star player for Paterson East Side, was dashing for the goal line to score the winning touchdown. But West Orange's Jimmy Sheeran stepped up and stopped Doby right on the goal line, securing a victory for West Orange High School. Larry Doby would courageously follow in the footsteps of Jackie Robinson and go on to achieve stardom. He became the first black baseball player in the American League in 1947 with the Cleveland Indians. Jimmy Sheeran would also exhibit courage and bravery, but his road would take a much different path.

Only two years after graduating from West Orange High School, Jimmy was a member of the 101st Airborne Division of paratroopers known as the "screaming eagles." In the predawn hours of June 6, 1944, he jumped behind German lines in the allies' D-day invasion of Normandy, France. Landing somewhere in between confusion and chaos, within twenty-four hours, Jimmy found himself captured by the Germans. Things didn't go according to plan, and many of his fellow paratroopers had already been killed. He certainly was lucky to be alive, and much uncertainty would lie ahead, with his fate in the hands of a desperate German army. As the next few days passed, he found himself being transferred at gunpoint farther behind enemy lines. He was transported in unmarked trucks lacking the required Red Cross symbol and fired upon by Allied aircraft, thinking it was German soldiers, and many of his fellow prisoners were killed by the strafing machine-gun fire.

Jimmy soon found himself packed like cattle into a closed boxcar on a train headed to a POW camp somewhere in the heart of Germany. Opportunity presented itself for an escape, and Jimmy made a daring leap from the speeding train. Jimmy and another man were badly bruised but fortunate to survive. Starving and thirsty, they ran until dawn, uncertain if they were in France or Germany. They had the good fortune of being

Jimmy Sheeran (44, front row) with his 1941 West Orange High School football team. *Author's collection.*

captured by the French underground resistance forces. After gaining their rescuers' trust and confidence, Jimmy and his fellow escapee continued their fight against the Nazis with the French underground. However, after a few weeks, Jimmy was once again forced to flee through the French countryside with the Germans in pursuit. He eluded capture and in a short time found himself in the small French town of Domrémy. By a miraculous coincidence, it was the birthplace of his mother living back in West Orange. He actually took refuge with his cousins, who helped conceal him from the Germans.

He was eventually reunited with the Americans of General Patton's advancing army through France. He returned safely to England but refused to be sent back home to West Orange and chose to be reunited with his unit. He then participated in Operation Market Garden from September 17 to 25, 1944. This was the Allied plan to strike Germany's industrial heartland, making large-scale use of airborne forces. The tactical objectives were to secure German-held bridges in the occupied Netherlands. This would allow a rapid ground advance by armored units into northern Germany. The mission ultimately failed, as depicted in the 1977 film *A Bridge Too Far*.

In December 1944, Jimmy and the men of the 101st Airborne were hopelessly surrounded by Germans in the small Belgian town of Bastogne at strategic crossroads. He was wounded in combat by exploding shrapnel, and all seemed lost. The soldiers at Bastogne hung on, refused to surrender and were eventually liberated by American forces. Jimmy once again overcame the odds and was rescued and returned safely to England. Jimmy miraculously survived the war and returned home a humble war hero. He served as West Orange mayor from 1958 to 1966 and insurance commissioner of New Jersey from 1974 to 1982 before he passed away in 2007 at the age of eighty-four.

Theodore Roosevelt once wrote, "Far better to dare mighty things and fail…then to take refuge with those who dwell in the dim twilight that knows neither victory nor defeat." Jimmy Sheeran was a young West Orange boy who dared mighty things, refused to accept defeat and forever dwelled in the light of victory.

West Orange Boy Salutes Eisenhower

Shortly after his triumphal return following World War II, General Eisenhower visited the Panama Canal Zone as general of the army in 1946. It was during this visit that my late uncle Private First Class Bill Fagan encountered the D-day commander in a chance meeting that neither would soon forget.

William "Bill" Fagan was born on February 22, 1928, in West Orange. He was too young to have served in World War II and was only fourteen when his eldest brother, my father and my grandfather joined the U.S. Navy in 1942. With Bill's brother and father gone, he remained at home with his mother, two older sisters and a younger brother.

In July 1945, shortly after his discharge from the navy, my grandfather opened Fagan's Texaco on the West Orange/Livingston border. My uncle Bill then went to work for his father at the gas station. When my father, Jim, returned home from the navy in January 1946, he didn't have much interest in working there. However, Uncle Bill was drafted in 1946, so my father joined my grandfather at Fagan's Texaco, only intending to work there while his brother Bill was away in the army.

Left to right: Bill Fagan, James Fagan Sr. and James Fagan Jr. at Fagan's Texaco shortly after Bill's return from the U.S. Army. *Author's collection.*

Uncle Bill was one of the last draftees out of West Orange. The draft had been abolished, and service in the peacetime army had become strictly volunteer-based. One of the first decisions facing Uncle Bill as a soldier was whether he should change his status from draftee to regular army by enlisting. As a draftee, he was only obligated to serve for one year. However, as an enlisted man, he would have to serve an additional year and be away from home for a total of two years. My grandfather advised Uncle Bill that no matter what they promised him, he should not sign the papers to enlist.

Uncle Bill was asked several times to enlist but always refused, wishing to keep his status as draftee. The issue finally came to a head at Camp Kilmer in New Jersey when Major Falls asked Uncle Bill to enlist. Adhering to the advice of my grandfather, he still refused. Major Falls informed Uncle Bill in no uncertain terms that if he didn't enlist, he would assign him to some faraway outpost, a place where he would be forgotten and maybe never heard from again. Uncle Bill was unfazed by the major's remarks and still refused to enlist. The next day, he found his assignment listed as APO 86. Uncle Bill asked a fellow soldier where it was, and the soldier replied, "Who did you tick off to get that post?"

APO 86, as it turned out, was far out in the South Pacific on the island of Iwo Jima taken by the U.S. Marines in February 1945. Uncle Bill began to wonder if perhaps Major Falls was right. Would he ever be heard from again?

Uncle Bill shipped out from Hoboken, New Jersey, on August 8, 1946, en route to Iwo Jima. By August 28, he found himself in the Atlantic port of Cristobal on the Panama Canal. As fate would have it, General Eisenhower was also visiting there at that time. Uncle Bill and a fellow soldier, Charlie Pilser of Brooklyn, were eating and relaxing in an empty rec hall when all of a sudden, a door sprang opened. A contingent of army brass led by a few muscular MPs and General Eisenhower suddenly and unexpectedly appeared. Both Uncle Bill and Charlie Pilser were stunned and caught off guard. Uncle Bill had a hamburger in one hand and a beer in the other and upon seeing General Eisenhower had to think and act quickly. There was no table around to put the hamburger and beer down so he placed the hamburger in his mouth and proudly saluted the general with his free hand and the other still holding the beer. Eisenhower, upon seeing this, stopped dead in his tracks and couldn't believe his eyes. He looked at Uncle Bill and remarked that this was a first for him as a general. Eisenhower stated that he had been saluted by countless thousands of soldiers, but none with a hamburger in his mouth. Apparently amused by the encounter, Eisenhower politely invited Uncle Bill and Charlie Pilser to join him on stage while he addressed the troops. The general then continued on his way, momentarily followed by both privates in disbelief of their good fortune. They, however, didn't get very far. As they started to walk behind General Eisenhower, one stout-looking MP with a devilish grin and billy club across his chest stepped up, blocking the paths of both men. He looked Uncle Bill and Charile Pilser in the eyes and said, "You guys ain't going nowhere."

It was all over in the blink of an eye as Eisenhower vanished from sight. Uncle Bill never did enlist and eventually made it back from Iwo Jima and was never forgotten. Neither was his memorable encounter with General Eisenhower, who eventually became our thirty-fourth president and perhaps was never again saluted by a soldier with a hamburger in his mouth.

Father Follows in Son's Footsteps and Joins Navy

Countless scores of West Orange residents answered the call of duty during World War II as the country faced an uncertain future. No family seemed to be immune from the surge of patriotism and pride in the national sentiment. As world events unfolded, many understood the unselfish struggle that lay ahead. It was not uncommon to have brothers or members of the same family in uniform. However, my father and grandfather found themselves in a unique situation, becoming the only father and son both serving during the war from West Orange.

My father, James Fagan Jr., graduated from West Orange High School in 1939. During the Depression years, most families struggled financially and could not afford college tuition. Following graduation, my father worked briefly as a messenger boy for Western Union before being employed at the General Electric plant in nearby Bloomfield in late 1939. My father and his friends were gathered at the corner of Main Street and Eagle Rock Avenue on December 7, 1941, when news came of Japan's attack on Pearl Harbor. West Orange boys quickly enlisted in all branches of the service and were soon off to war, some never to return home again.

In June 1942, my father enlisted in the United States Navy. He attended boot camp at Newport, Rhode Island, and by the end of July 1942 was undergoing specialized training at Perdue University in Lafayette, Indiana. In January 1943, he qualified for sea duty with a rank of electricians mate third class and was sent to Miami, Florida, to await further orders.

His father, my grandfather, James Fagan Sr., also served in the United States Navy during World War II. He enlisted in the navy at age forty-one in August 1942, two full months after his eldest son, James. He had left his wife, Jennie, my grandmother, with four younger children at their home on 14 North Park Drive in West Orange. He also left his job at the Walter Kidde Company in Belleview to join the navy. My grandfather also attended boot camp in Newport, Rhode Island, where my father had been only months before. After boot camp, my grandfather was assigned to Guantanamo Bay in Cuba with the rank of carpenters mate third class. It was a bit unusual to have a father follow in his son's footsteps during World War II, but it happened in West Orange.

What actually motivated James J. Fagan Sr. to enlist in the United States Navy during World War II will never be known. He was forty-one years old and born too late to have served in World War I like his elder brother Jack. Perhaps his call to duty was driven by guilt or a

West Orange reunion following boot camp in 1942. *Left to right*: daughter Betty, wife Jennie, James Fagan Sr., sister Maggie, daughter Peggy and son Richard in front. *Author's collection.*

sense of adventure. Maybe he saw this as his only opportunity to serve his country. Perhaps he was inspired by the scores of young men from West Orange—including his eldest son, James—who went off to war. However, one thing for certain is that at his age, he didn't have to go. In doing so, he placed the responsibility of his young family squarely on the shoulders of his wife, Jennie. Without her love and support, his service in the navy would likely not have been possible. It certainly must have been an emotional farewell for Jennie, seeing both her husband and son off to war in service of the United States Navy.

With my grandfather in the U.S. Navy, word had come to my father in Miami that the newly commissioned sub chaser USS PC 608, headed for the South Pacific, had an opening for an electricians mate third class. Both

Naval Reunion

Petty Officers Fagan Meet at Southern Base

So Third Class Petty Officer Jim Fagan of West Orange walked over to Third Class Petty Officer Jim Fagan of West Orange. "Hello, Jim," one said. "Hello, dad," the other replied.

It was a meeting of father and son. Their home is at 14 North Park drive. They recently met at a Southern naval base for the first time since Jim Jr. entered service last June. When his ship docked, he hustled out to look for his dad, who enlisted in August. The first person the son saw when he entered the recreation hall was Jim Sr.

The father received the petty officer's rating when he enlisted. His son trained at Purdue University, then received his rating. Mrs. Fagan, who received word of the meeting this week, said her husband was home on leave five months ago, but her son has not been home since shortly after he entered the Navy.

The reunion of James Fagan Jr. (left) and James Fagan Sr., (right) at Guantanamo Bay Cuba also made news back home. *Author's collection.*

my father and another sailor wanted the position. My father had especially wanted to get on board because the ship was stopping at Guantanamo Bay in Cuba where my grandfather was already stationed. He had not seen his father in nearly six months and was very anxious for this unique opportunity. My father secured the assignment aboard the ship by winning the toss of a coin. This ship would be his home for the next three years. On January 7, 1943, the USS PC 608 dropped anchor in the harbor at Guantanamo Bay, Cuba. Father and son were soon happily reunited, both as sailors serving in the United States Navy. This unusual news also appeared in newspapers back home, but for security reasons, the reunion was only listed as being at a southern naval base.

The relatively safe and secure surroundings of Guantanamo Bay in Cuba were not where my grandfather wanted to be. He was dissatisfied with his role as a ship painter and made several requests to the base commander to be transferred aboard ship for sea duty. He was likely denied because of his age and family responsibilities back home. But while my father's ship had stopped in port, the base commander at Guantanamo Bay discreetly called him into his office. He wanted to discuss the requests my grandfather had been making for sea duty. Apparently, the base commander was reluctantly willing to approve James Sr.'s request and wanted to see what his son had to say. James Jr. explained to the base commander that his father was stubborn and not likely to stop requesting sea duty, so the commander might as well grant the approval for transfer. The base commander was relieved to hear that James Sr.'s son and family had no objections. It was the toss of a coin that bought James Jr. to Guantanamo Bay to be reunited with his father. The same toss of the coin also had far-reaching effects, because after the base commander discussed the situation with James Jr., he subsequently approved sea duty for James Fagan Sr. But my grandfather would have to wait almost two more years to get his chance aboard ship.

James Fagan Sr. finally received his assignment for sea duty in early November 1944. He was transferred to the USS *Apollo* (AS-25), a sub tender headed for the South Pacific as it stopped in Guantanamo Bay en route to the Panama Canal. Once aboard ship, James Fagan Sr. sailed through the Panama Canal as the ship continued on to Pearl Harbor. In December 1944, the ship set a course for Guam in the Mariana Islands, where it provided services to various submarines of the United States Pacific Fleet. James Fagan Sr. got his chance for sea duty and adventure on the high seas, though he soon left the ship and was honorably discharged from the navy on May 26, 1945, only months before the Japanese surrender in September 1945.

James Fagan Sr. served a total of two years, nine months and sixteen days in the United States Navy during World War II. He was never engaged in combat, likely was never in harms way and likely never even saw the enemy. But his answer to the call of duty speaks volumes to his sense of patriotism, despite the fact that it created hardship for his family in West Orange. Upon returning home, he used his mustering out pay to open Fagan's Texaco gas station at the corner of Old Short Hills Road and Northfield Avenue. My father and his younger brother Bill continued Fagan's Texaco until the business was sold in 1979. Five of his grandchildren—including myself—would eventually work at the gas station at various times. James

Sketch by fellow crew member of James Fagan Jr. (above) napping on top of a twenty-millimeter ammunition box aboard the USS PC 608. Wartime photo of James Fagan Jr. is seen to the right. *Author's collection.*

Fagan Sr. passed away on September 29, 1965, and was instrumental in first introducing me to West Orange history.

My father, James Jr., eventually served for two more years aboard the USS PC 608, performing convoy escort duty. Following Germany's surrender, he was reassigned to his second ship, the USS *Chimariko*, a seagoing tug heading for the South Pacific. Up to this time, he had never encountered the enemy, but his new shipmates and himself were overly anxious to have some memorable stories to one day tell their children before war's end. As the saying goes, be careful what you wish for.

August 15, 1945, started like any other day for the *Chimariko* heading for the Marshall Islands on its way to Okinawa. A radio dispatch had informed the ship that hostilities with Japan had ceased pending surrender negations. The war was over, and the planned invasion of Japan, which had been in the preliminary stages, would now not be necessary, saving countless lives. But it also meant no more chances for many sailors like my father, who were still eager to fight.

Unexpectedly, during the early part of October 1945, to the southwest of Okinawa, a dangerous typhoon had begun sweeping past Saipan and into the Philippine Sea. As the storm grew violent, it raced northward, kicking up waves sixty feet high with sustained winds at 150 miles per hour. In its path at sea lay countless unprepared vessels of the U.S. Navy, including the USS *Chimariko*, with my father aboard.

He was on duty in the engine room when Typhoon Louise hit the small two-hundred-foot vessel. The ship was being tossed violently about and began rapidly taking on water down the bulkheads into the engine room. James Jr. had not yet reached his twenty-fifth birthday but now found himself responsible for the diesel electrical generators supplying the ship's power. The ship's captain gave the order to maintain power by any means necessary. Without electric power, the crew would be at the mercy of the sea and face an unspeakable fate. My father often told me that he really didn't know what to do but just placed oily rags over the generator panel to protect it as best he could from the incoming seawater. Miraculously, his quick thinking worked, and the bilge pumps held fast as the ship maintained power throughout the deadly struggle.

The crew members never engaged the enemy but got their story as they fought and won their battle with the sea. My father lived the rest of his life beaming with immeasurable pride about his World War II service. The United States Navy crushed two enemy fleets at once, receiving their surrenders only four months apart. They brought our land-based air power within range of the enemy and set our ground forces on the beachheads to achieve the final victory. James Fagan Sr. and James Fagan Jr. were forever proud of their supporting roles as father and son. I personally watched my father peacefully weigh anchor on April 7, 2003, on his final voyage as he set sail into eternity. The last words we ever exchanged with each other on his deathbed were "I love you," leaving no unfinished business between us. His youthful spirit will forever symbolically ride the high seas just beyond the horizon, where the world will just never know about its greatest heroes.

BIBLIOGRAPHY

Articles

Brennan, Joseph. "Orange Mountain Cable Railway, Orange Mountain Traction Company." *Destinations 27: The Newsletter of the North Jersey Electric Railway Historical Society* 14, no. 1 (June 1999).

"For Rest and Convalescence." *American Journal of Nursing* 8 (1908).

Maxwell, Anna C. "Letters to the Editor: The Haven Country Club." *American Journal of Nursing* 14 (1914).

"Private Railroad to Move a Mountain." *Railway Age* 167, no. 18 (November 10, 1969).

Taylor, Herbert L. "The Orange Mountain Traction Lines." *NRHS Bulletin* (June/July 1943).

Underwood, John. "Amos Stagg: A Century of Honesty." *Sports Illustrated*, August 13, 1962.

"We Have a Very Long History with Brown Brothers Harriman." *Alumni Magazine: Columbia University Presbyterian Hospital School of Nursing Alumni Association, Inc.* 105, no. 1 (Summer 2012).

Books

Biographical and Genealogical History of the City of Newark and Essex County. New York: Lewis Publishing Company, 1898.

BIBLIOGRAPHY

The Blue Book or Elite Directory of Orange, East Orange, West Orange, South Orange. Orange, NJ: Baldwin Publishing Company, 1892.

Brown, John Crosby. *A Hundred Years of Merchant Banking.* New York: privately printed, 1909.

Brown, Mary Elizabeth. *St. Cloud Church.* West Orange, NJ: privately published, 1917.

Considine, Bob. *The Unconstructed Amateur.* San Francisco: Amos Alonzo Stagg Foundation Inc., 1962.

Constitution, By-Laws, Officers and Members of the Essex County Country Club. Orange, NJ: Essex County Country Club, 1920.

Essex County Social Register 1930. Newark, NJ: Rofflow C. Blackmer Publisher, 1930.

Fagan, Joseph. *Eagle Rock Reservation.* Charleston, SC: Arcadia Publishing, 2002.

———. *West Orange.* Charleston, SC: Arcadia Publishing, 2009.

Healy, John M. *A Time Remembered: West Orange during the Depression and War Years.* Ormond Beach, FL: Corporate Image Publishing, 1993.

Hutchings, David W. *Edison at Work.* New York: Hastings House Publishers, 1969.

Lash, Joseph P. *Eleanor and Franklin.* New York: W.W. Norton and Company, Inc., 1971.

Lee, Francis Bazley. *Genealogical and Memorial History of the State of New Jersey.* New York: Lewis Historical Publishing Company, 1910.

McHugh, Michael. *George B. McClellan the Disposable Patriot.* Arlington Heights, IL: Christian Liberty Press, 1998.

Pierson, David Lawrence. *History of the Oranges to 1921.* New York: Lewis Historical Publishing Company, 1922.

Sears, Stephen W. *The Civil War Papers of George B. McClellan.* New York: Ticknor and Fields, 1989.

———. *George B. McClellan the Young Napoleon.* New York: Ticknor and Fields, 1988.

Shaw, William H. *History of Essex and Hudson Counties, New Jersey.* Philadelphia: Everts and Peck, 1884.

Sheeran, James J. *No Surrender: A World War II Memoir.* New York: Berkley Caliber, 2011.

Syrett, Harold C. *The Gentleman and the Tiger.* Philadelphia: J.P. Lippincott Company, 1956.

Whittemore, Henry. *The Founders and Builders of the Oranges.* Newark, NJ: L.J. Hardham, Printer and Bookbinder, 1896.

Wirth, Edward. *Thomas Edison at Work in West Orange.* Charleston, SC: Arcadia Publishing, 2008.

BIBLIOGRAPHY

Libraries

Houghton Library, Harvard University, Cambridge, MA
Newark Public Library
Orange Public Library
Princeton University Library, Princeton, NJ
West Orange Public Library

Newspapers

Newark Evening News
New York Times
Orange Chronicle
Orange Journal
West Orange Chronicle
West Orange Weekly Review

Other Resources

Ciamillo, Elmer "Sonny." Personal interviews, West Orange, NJ, 2011–2014.

Duenkel, Ginny. Phone interview, Stanhope, NJ, 2010.

Fagan, James, Jr. Personal interviews, West Orange, NJ, 1965–2007.

Fagan, James, Sr. Personal diary, West Orange, NJ, 1925.

Fagan, William. Personal interviews, Mt. Pocono, PA, 1965–2013.

Healy, John. Personal interviews, West Orange, NJ, 2010–2013.

Horn, Don, Sr.. Personal interviews, West Orange, NJ, 2012–2013.

Piccolo, Don. Personal interviews, New York, NY, 2005–2007.

Pran, Dith. Personal interview, West Orange, NJ, 2002.

Raymond, Doug. E-mail correspondence, Stanhope, NJ, 2011–present

Robertson, Dorothy. Personal interview, St. Louis, MO, 2010.

Stagg, Robert. Phone interview, Stanhope, NJ, 2012.

Tinquist, Kenneth. Personal interviews, West Orange, NJ, 1965–present.

ABOUT THE AUTHOR

Joseph Fagan is the fourth generation of his family to have grown up in West Orange. He developed an interest in local history at a young age and has spent a lifetime researching the town where his roots run deep. This is his third book on West Orange history, which contains stories from his weekly newspaper articles that he has been writing consecutively since April 2009. He has given frequent lectures on town history at the West Orange Public Library and received the honorary title of official historian of the township of West

Orange in 2012 from the mayor and town council. In January 2014, he began hosting a monthly local cable TV show, *Discover West Orange*, focusing on town history. He resides in Sussex County, New Jersey, with his wife, Debbie, also from West Orange, whom he met at Mountain High School in 1974, and they have one son, Joseph. Professionally Fagan is a State of New Jersey Licensed Master Plumber and has been self-employed for the last twenty-six years.